# so that you know

**Also by Mani Rao**

*The Essential Kalidasa*

*Bhagavad Gita: God's Song*

*Saundarya Lahari: Wave of Beauty*

manirao.com

# so that you know

## mani rao

HarperCollins *Publishers* India

First published in India by HarperCollins *Publishers* 2025
HarperCollins *Publishers* India, Cyber City, Building 10-A,
Gurugram, Haryana-122002, India
www.harpercollins.co.in

2 4 6 8 10 9 7 5 3 1

Copyright © Mani Rao Foundation 2025

P-ISBN: 978-93-6989-017-0
E-ISBN: 978-93-6989-797-1

Mani Rao asserts the moral right
to be identified as the author of this work.

All rights reserved. No part of this publication may be reproduced,
stored in a retrieval system, or transmitted, in any form or by any means,
electronic, mechanical, photocopying, recording or otherwise,
without the prior permission of the publishers.

Without limiting the exclusive rights of any author, contributor or the
publisher of this publication, any unauthorized use of this publication to
train generative artificial intelligence (AI) technologies is expressly prohibited.
HarperCollins also exercise their rights under Article 4(3) of the Digital Single
Market Directive 2019/790 and expressly reserve this publication from the text
and data-mining exception.

Typeset in 11.5/15 Aldine401 BT at
HarperCollins *Publishers* India

Printed and bound at
Replika Press Pvt. Ltd.

This book is produced from independently certified FSC® paper to ensure
responsible forest management.

★

HarperCollins *Publishers*, Macken House, 39/40 Mayor Street Upper,
Dublin 1, D01 C9W8, Ireland

# Praise

'Often enigmatic, always exquisitely shaped, the poems in Mani Rao's *So That You Know* introduce us to an ensemble of previous and future selves. Except that we can't always tell which is which. Despite the promise of fair warning in its title, this collection does not prepare us for the everyday reality that its pensive, urbane poems transfigure into a minefield of anomaly and dissonance. *So That You Know* confronts us with fruit that resist etiquette, with vistas of a mutable world of hazard and tremor, eyed warily over the edge of a coffee mug. Dwelling on a mother's cabinet of fears for her daughter, for instance, Rao writes: "*No wonder I am so fearless / All the panic safe with her.*" Objects, places, animals, limbs—all these show a tendency, at once alarming and delightful, to run, hide, change places and alter themselves here. At the core of this book lies a generative tension between presence and persona, essential to the lifelong project of self-fashioning, with all its attendant risks. How do we know who to be, these poems ask us. Mani Rao's *So That You Know* is a wry, witty and bracing instruction manual in both defining, and defying, oneself.'

—**Ranjit Hoskote**

'Mani Rao is the least metaphysical of our poets, or to put it another way, the most material. Her very myths have the quality of concrete fables. In her newest poems, she offers up a body—her own?—preparing for erasure. Naturally, ghosts are a worry: not the spooks of metaphysics, but the traces of matter bodies leave, or simply disclose in the wash of their absence. *"Black hair emerges / on the other side // as a palette of grey, / then vanishes / in white light."* Black and white and grey recur with almost heraldic import; bled of colour, graphics hammer the message home. One image is simply a mouth created by a pair of lips impressed on the page, floating there like a mocking black hole. Rupture dogs rapture. The detritus of marriage is viewed from a great—even galactic—distance (and worth two minutes' silence). Things are seen for what they are: A monster owl on the fence flew away. What is it the sign of? The sign of an owl. Rao is not altogether lost to abstraction, can still discover a winged heart in her chest, but she has returned to the only self she can trust—alone is the soma of song. She allows herself the pleasures of sardony in the occasional toss-off at Iowa or India, even a pun on her name, but the mood remains defiant, the temperature low: *"It is Antarctica I need."* One secret she will share: *"God is a shy bird."* And one piece of advice: *"Be wildered."* Scrupulous, savage, fearless: here is poetry that refuses to beguile. We owe it our complete attention.'

—**Irwin Allan Sealy**

'I love the gentle whip-crack of both line and image in Mani Rao's poems. There is some precious gift in the intensity of such condensed language, that tells truth sparely and evocatively, so that a reader could rise to meet and know it. Eunice de Souza had that gift, and Kamala Das, and Shreela Ray. So does Mani Rao.'

—**Kazim Ali**

'Unscared of the sacred, wearing grief wryly, *So That You Know* sets the epic in conversation with the intimate at the same table, knives out, sharpened inward. This incisive paean to the cardinal humanity of love and loss demonstrates why Mani Rao is a uniquely masterful voice in Indian letters and world poetry today.'
—**Alvin Pang**

'Assured and playful, typographically agile and semantically spare, this is quintessential Mani Rao poetic terrain. This volume offers a glimpse of a thoughtful and dedicated poet's journey over the years.'
—**Arundhathi Subramaniam**

'In *So That You Know,* Mani Rao's tour de force of new and selected poems, readers will find themselves in thrilling encounters with the hinge upon which all living things swing. In poems spanning nearly forty years, Rao engages a negative capability that serves as both an ethics and a warning against false promise of closure; poems that prove, in their meticulous attention, that the conditions by which you learn to live today, will not be those that are needed tomorrow: "*When wings are ready / the bird has flown ...*" ("Conditions of Freedom"). Via self-erasure, in the remnant of rhyme and metre, via essay in its purest form of finding ("I, Lorine Niedecker") and always via the tender luminosity of the lyric and an expansive sense of humour, Mani Rao gives us poems that suggest it is via acceptance of indeterminacy that we find ... dare I say it? Freedom. "*When I walked into a poem / and met a meticulous metre // Got battered by drums / that drowned the lyrics // I couldn't tell the theme / for the scheme and // bum-rush end-rhymes / crashed my dreams // Maybe I ought to mince / my words, toe the line // But I don't / I'm a freedom fighter* ("Vers Libre").'
—**Claudia Keelan**

# Contents

| | |
|---|---|
| *Preface* | xv |
| **So That You Know** | 1 |
| Did I Mention | 3 |
| This Marriage | 4 |
| That Marriage | 5 |
| Table Manners | 6 |
| Tomatoes Reply | 7 |
| How I Knew | 9 |
| My Corner | 10 |
| I'm Not Afraid of Death, I'm Afraid | 11 |
| Some of What I Learned from Books | 12 |
| Just Looking | 13 |
| Invoice | 15 |
| Crumbs | 16 |
| Statutory Warning | 17 |
| Happily M | 18 |
| Retrospective | 19 |
| Divorce Blooms | 20 |
| Waiheke Within | 22 |
| Island | 23 |

| | |
|---|---|
| If Only | 26 |
| Not Fair | 27 |
| So Yes, but No | 28 |
| Tryst | 29 |
| Bolero | 30 |
| Thick | 31 |
| Vacay On Myrtle Beach | 32 |
| Season's Greetings: A Found Poem | 33 |
| Love Poem at 3.33 a.m. | 34 |
| My Old Woman | 35 |
| Reading Her [Writing | 36 |
| Story Moon | 41 |
| If It's Any Consolation | 42 |
| Waiting For Gold | 43 |
| Poem For a Librarian | 44 |
| What Are Grown-Ups Made Of | 45 |
| Were I A Wizard There Would Be | 46 |
| Doobie Doobie Doo | 47 |
| If We Live Long Enough, We Shall | 48 |
| Vers Libre | 49 |
| Conditions of Freedom | 50 |
| A Little Secret | 51 |
| Fusion 2024 | 53 |
| Postcard from India | 54 |
| Iowa Romancing | 56 |
| This Week's Mosquito | 57 |
| War | 58 |

| | |
|---|---:|
| Finding Family | 59 |
| Safe | 60 |
| Transfusion | 61 |
| On Your Lost Taste of Banganapalle | 62 |
| Without Touching | 64 |
| The Dotted Line | 65 |
| Advanced Lessons | 66 |
| Writing on the Wall | 67 |
| No Souvenir | 68 |
| April 13, 2006 | 69 |
| Death Has My Back | 70 |
| See, No Leaves | 71 |
| Pathetic Fallacy | 72 |
| Law of Physics | 73 |
| Suraj, the Boatman | 74 |
| Kashi Triptych | 75 |
| Not For Sale | 79 |
| Tiruvannamalai | 81 |
| Of the Monkeys of Vrindavan | 82 |
| I Talk to Myself—I Talk to You | 83 |
| I, Lorine Niedecker | 86 |
| **Sing to Me** | **93** |
| Sing to Me | 95 |
| Peace Treaty | 98 |
| Father's Day | 99 |
| My Daughter Philomela | 101 |
| Cadmus Is History | 103 |

| | |
|---|---|
| Jove's Collar | 105 |
| As Promised Tithonus | 106 |
| Postcard Aphrodite | 107 |
| Fêted | 111 |
| Ding-Dong Bell | 115 |
| Iliad Blues | 116 |
| In the Shower, Thinking of Actaeon | 117 |
| Aphrodite: | 118 |
| On the Tail | 119 |
| Venus and Adonis | 120 |
| Or Us | 121 |
| Simile | 122 |
| Cupid and Psyche | 123 |
| Midas, a Casino in Vegas | 124 |
| Poem, Sisyphus | 125 |
| Ouranos Returns | 127 |

*from* **Ghostmasters (2010)**   129

| | |
|---|---|
| Bird Signs | 131 |
| Classic | 132 |
| Location | 133 |
| Drought | 135 |
| Catching Up | 136 |
| Choose | 138 |
| Tensile | 139 |
| Drowning by Numbers | 140 |
| Epitaph | 142 |

| | |
|---|---|
| Star-Crossed | 145 |
| Sporous | 146 |
| Address | 147 |
| Five-Word Poem | 148 |
| End of Scene | 149 |
| Airing at a Sniff | 151 |
| Grand Finale | 152 |
| Shots | 153 |
| Shorts | 155 |
| Duet | 156 |
| Sequence | 157 |
| Haul | 158 |
| Slough | 160 |
| Pupa | 162 |
| Worker | 163 |
| Auditorium | 165 |
| Writing to Stop | 167 |
| Geocity | 171 |
| Bird Union | 173 |
| Ebru | 174 |
| Chorus | 175 |
| Möbius | 176 |
| Void Plate | 177 |
| Other | 179 |
| Pol Pot | 180 |
| § | 182 |

| | |
|---|---:|
| Ɵ | 184 |
| ∞ | 186 |
| Calling | 187 |
| *from* **Echolocation (2003)** | 191 |
| *from* **Salt (2000)** | 219 |
| *from* **The Last Beach (1999)** | 231 |
| *from* **Living Shadows (1997)** | 249 |
| *from* **Catapult Season (1993)** | 261 |
| *from* **Wingspan (1987)** | 283 |
| Credits | 291 |

# Preface

At a reading, once, a reader asked me—'*Have you always been like that?*' My response—an exclamation mark hanging in a sentence of gaping no words. To what '*that*' could they have been referring? Lines from my poems rushed through my mind. If I said *yes*, I may have owned up to a crime I had not committed. If I said, 'No-no, *these* are just poems,' I would risk sounding like a traitor to Poetry.

*These* may be anything, maybe facsimiles, maybe phantasms—you, dear reader, cannot reach out and pinch them. Much easier to consider all narratives about characters and incidents fictitious and any resemblance to reality, pure coincidence. *One day, someone goes in search of the fictitious place in my story and finds it.*

The assumption in the reader's question, and in my non-affirming non-denial, also raises an ethical problem. Who has not been accused by family and friends of pilfering private moments and using them in a poem or story? Or of regretting bouts of contentment for how that starves creativity? *We don't see each other anymore / Was it art for art's sake / Or did we get some poems out of it.*

Do you really think that I really think experience exists to serve poems? Expect me to plead 'not guilty' to such disrespect.

Although, I murmur, where would history be without such crimes? We need record-keepers, archives, alibis. Oh, we need entire news reports, even live relays.

Does taking a photograph of a person in distress interfere with helping that person? Is it not inhumane, or just insensitive, to expose anguish, and a sick fetish to bare one's own anguish?

Imagine Gauguin's *Self-Portrait*—a medical emergency until those brushstrokes made art. And who says life and art exclude each other? You can be Florence Nightingale exuding genuine compassion, and still feed the scene you witnessed to dark comedy. You are multitudes.

Isn't it better to write poems about *topics*? On the dazzle of rice, for instance. Some reader will still read my life on those rice grains and make that mistake—*were you always like that*?

But these days I'm craving privacy even from myself. So That You Know.

—**Mani Rao**
Bangalore, 2025

# so that you know

# Did I Mention

Did I mention how I see us

Heads too large for our child bodies
Mouth-buds, wide-set eyes

Like Charlie Brown and Lucy

Walking, blowing
Soap bubbles, speech blurbs

Who's buried under the memory tree
What's the name of the bird in that nest

Tell no one how old we are
Or that we know Chiquitita by heart

# This Marriage

It's not too cold, I know,
but I had nowhere else

to keep this overcoat

All my suitcases were full
And my closet overcrowded

So I just let it sit
upon my shoulders

# That Marriage

A haunted house
afraid to die

Echoes fold

Should the poem end there

The Happy Prince returns
on the radio

'Swallow, little swallow, will you not
stay with me one night longer'

# Table Manners

Why can't a watermelon

Seeds copious like
a lake full of fish,

dead, fins
poking gloss

Be more like a papaya
Beads rounded up

Scrape-easy

# Tomatoes Reply

There are three kinds of people, I was told.

Those who take advice, those who learn from others' errors,
those who only realize when shit happens to them.

I ate that scolding. Called her later from the grocery.
Let her know of three types of tomatoes.

Red all over, thick-skinned. Pesticides make them good
for photographs or soups.

Orangeish yellowish plucked green then gassed.
Tasteless, but a dash of lemon does wonders.

And those ripened on the vine. Expensive, but, I said,
I would like salad today.

# How I Knew

It was you

Not because you said it was
Not you

Or that you don't even know
the word I heard you say

But that I told you of
my dream

Over the rim of my
coffee cup

First thing this
morning

Accusingly

# My Corner

Now that I live on a dead end street
The good deeds of my past life
return as a cat

She patrols the unmarked fence
and invisible gate
between the T-junction
and my territory

When intruders turn my way,
this bullet darts right to left
ominously

A misanthrope cat may be
a tautology

Maybe the street went someplace
once and never returned

Maybe shook hands
with other streets
and changed its course

Be what may
Run, feet, run

# I'm Not Afraid of Death, I'm Afraid

Of inconsequential sunsets, of
fingerprints on spectacle lenses,
and always waking up at 3.33

# Some of What I Learned from Books

Give books away before they gather mold.
Will I be lucky or live to be old?

So you were fooled by the cover.
You're the fool and it's also over.

Not all great poets find renown.
Oh the snoring when they sleep on their own.

# Just Looking

**There's no love** in my right pocket
**There's no love** in my left pocket
There's no love in my cleavage
**There's no love** in my back pocket
There's no love in my handbag
There's no love in my wallet
**There's no love** in the shoebox
There's no love in the closet
There's no love in the inbox
There's no love in the spam
**There's no love** in the shopping cart
There's no love in the trash
**There's no love** behind curtains
**There's no love** under the carpet
**There's no love** in the refrigerator
**There's no love** in the freezer
**There's no love** on the cutting board
There's no love in the pan
**There's no love** in the elevator

There's no love at the doorbell
There's no love when the gate opens
There's no love when the gate closes
There's no love if I look right
There's no love if I look left
There's no love across the street
There's no love in the parking lot
There's no love in the security cameras
There's no love if I roll up the window
There's no love if I roll down the window
There's no love on my plate
There's no love on the bill
There's no love to-go
                no love in skies clouds
                no love in grass always taller
In cattle fattening just because
In multiplication of insects
Over rotting tomatoes
In time-lapse flower shows
                      no love on a stormy night when banged by the wind the bees are having to walk
There's no love to be continued
                no love to stop

# Invoice

Doesn't stop. Is he

getting paid by
the word? Where

do I send the bill
for m y ears?

Borrows from his
deficit

I'm his World-
Bank

# Crumbs

Crown glued to scalp
Fist clenched on sceptre
You can tell he's King

A sword hangs upon his neck
Is that why his smile is meek
He smiles first he's King

Not as if he's wasting our money
Doesn't have keys to the treasury
How many treats can one man eat
Leave him alone he's King

# Statutory Warning

When the door shuts and the key
turns in wedlock it is said

Your entire life flashes
before your eyes

That you think it will end
keeps you going

Tomorrow,
next week,
year after

Dream of those open
days' inattentive smile

Old flames swarming
your slimmer version

But colours are too bright
Everyone's taking selfies

And you no longer smile
in photographs

# Happily M

The apple knows
of the worm

Blushing
for the tableau

Shows no sign
of what eats

Like a happily m
couple

Secrets buried
in the back garden

ferment

# Retrospective

Photographs of children born to others
Messages to missed understandings
To all the variables of past and future
Over a chipped coffee cup, let me be
A memory without gravity

# Divorce Blooms

Having drawn the knife
you flung it

The next morning
an algae bloom

swathed the island
Our island

How sea-creatures
must have rouged

their lips
upon our cuts

A second look at *The
New Zealand Herald*

And—a spill of Bordeaux
from the wine festival

Your ferry slides
into the cake

of Half Moon Bay
to carve you

a sweet slice
Happy Birthday!

# Waiheke Within

On full-moon nights gliding
from deck to garden

Sucked into an arching tunnel
of tea trees

Speeding over pronounced faces
of orchids

To the fallen pine breathing
mushroom stairwells

For the walk scratched downhill
to the beach.

The dunes will have moved
Coastline redrawn

And the wind will be trilling
fifty miles an hour.

Waiheke within.

Storm columns clang there.
Guttural histories

# Island

Someone is always stepping upon my long, invisible hair
I cough, and a voice will ask if I am all right
Oh to empty my bladder without an alibi

Alone is a substance I crave
Alone is the soma of song
I am always interested in some

I know how porcupines unleash their quills,
how turtles retreat
That's me opening a book at a random page
and staying that way
Books are my carapace
Taped to my closed door is a notice—
'I am not here'

You think you are in the middle of nowhere
Count ten and a person
will materialize
A shepherd, farm worker,
random person chewing a tamarind

It is Antarctica I need. Lines, curves.
Hemstitched curves rippling on snowscape.

To be the hallucination of a polar bear whose tracks haunt the
    paintings of Stephen Eastaugh who dreamt
of a cruise to Antarctica where he met a girl who looked me up
    on Wikipedia and revised my story
To disappear to myself in shelves of silence beyond duplicities
    of oceans and mountains of past and future lives of postures
    and readers
To be spun upon a sundial flash-reading the names of all the
    storms to be

When her father was in a coma, she visited him daily. Sat beside him and read him the newspaper headlines. Cross marks upon the dates. One day, she woke up and knew not to visit. An hour later, the nurse called. Her father. Gone. She felt ashamed. At her slowness. Father waiting and waiting for an alone morning.

The waiting is now clean
Body leans toward the door
Door foreshadows
Who lifts a mist why is the steed on a hillock
Figure tapering over it black and grey
Speechless as though the last breath can be saved
The floor is a mess

Tell me you're lonely I'll take you for a walk
where news of other islands dribbles ashore

Objects, whiffs
Strange seeds

Shells pirouette on pointed ends
Pellets radiate from crab burrows

Wind wheezes in foreign languages
Ankles itch from salty licks

I'll let you uncount with me
Giant trees of lightning
Waves in splinters
Ocean walled in
Seats full and standing room only
on sunken ships
You'll be evidence when
sky meets sea

Tell me you're lonely I'll
teach you to bite your nails

I'll bite your nails

# If Only

A bit inconvenient
To die just to drop

This sticky lover
That loveless parent

If only one could just get plastic surgery
Change lives behind the shrubbery

# Not Fair

I get older so
do you I
never catch

up you train me
for your death to

my patterns you do
patterns I want something

to shock you
My namesake tree

to drop all its leaves
in the centre of spring

Remind me what
I gain by being here

Love me in a hurry

# So Yes, but No

Like two rivers laden
with lands and legends

Sharp lights in leaf-boats
edging towards futures

of highlights on waves,
are we not

too substantial to meet
except in the ocean.

Me in my orbit, you in yours, always
inching closer while moving away.

Like two celestial objects, may we
revolve around each other.

In any room, there's only room
for a single poet. Take turns.

# Tryst

A nowhere place, mountains
and jungles, you say, but I picture
paparazzi, zoom lenses reading
our minds for their PhDs.

Germinated from the voltage
in our synapses, these eye-skies
inscribe us and bugs on-ground
record our ifs for finalities.

Easier if we were playing others.
As Antony-Cleopatra we could slip
a second kiss into the script
without consequence.

Message me where on blank paper
I'll say when in invisible ink

# Bolero

Advance one step
Retreat two

In seven days we are
Seven steps apart

In one month we are
Particles of dust

If you detect me
Reach out to pinch me

Between your thumb and
Forefinger

If I spot your sail on the horizon
I'll check the weather

# Thick

There comes a turn in the story of a pair of lovers
when mirages seem mirrors and visitors notice how
they now behave as one.

Encounter them and you enter a jungle, hallowed.
Slow down, one step at a time, lift each foot
by the knee.

Find yourself in a clearing, be wildered by diversity.
Space is an enclosure of trees, thick as thieves.

Roots tangled, branches locked.
A weed strangles a bough becomes a bridge upon a swamp
where animated rot grumbles.

What struggles and dies or survives, thrives, depends
on what, who knows, they are the dervish whirling,
and you, dust.

# Vacay On Myrtle Beach

Welcome to a beach town with mountains
of condos. Peak season year-round.

Every crevice on the crags booked in advance.
Retirees flock here to brood on mortality.

Higher floors are steep, obviously, although
you snag discounts with gambles on longevity.

We find a low floor with a salty balcony
to confront the ocean and contemplate
gulls' underbellies.

We're not snowbirds looking for a perch
Nor so old that we wonder who's first
There's winter in our hearts
Will thaw here

# Season's Greetings:
# A Found Poem

Peacocks make all kinds of calls:
At twilight, they fly up into the pine trees and the males call out to each other and to distant birds—'Helllllp hellllllllp!'

The peahens, on the other hand, sort of say 'hell-O, hell-O.'

Sometimes the males call out with a sad dove-like call 'Ohhhhh ohhhhh,' sometimes accompanied by the dogs howling too—all at neighbouring coyotes.

When the males are fanned out, and there are several around, they go 'Aaaaahhh Aaaaahhh Aaaaahhh,' maybe up to six times each, back and forth between each other.

If they are disturbed in the night, especially if the moon is up, they will call back and forth with the 'Aaaaahhh' calls. This all-night-calling only happens once or so in the breeding season.

Near the end of the mating season, their poor voices get hoarse, and sometimes they can be heard to bray or even squeak.

# Love Poem at 3.33 a.m.

I see her eyes in water
Suddenly the water is full of eyes
Splashing my face
I'm shy

        I tore out the wind chimes
        to listen
        You were racing through my veins
        The curtains did a two-step
        and swirled

I'm leaving you
Even in my dreams I'm leaving you
You don't believe me
Even in my dreams you don't believe me

# My Old Woman

When death fell asleep between my legs
One arm slung over my knee
I pulled her up to my leaking breasts
And heard her grind her teeth

                Does not inhabit herself
                Stun guns of solar hair and eye flash hide her age
                Born in a mirror in water precariously unheld
                Will never die

Sometimes runeface spreads
Wind wrinkling a lake
Dolphins flipping at eyes and mouth
Sometimes a crucifix
Nose the bent of spine
Splayed veins from eyebolts

# Reading Her [Writing

Facing her [back [easel [scene [

Backdrop: sleeping mountain-range
Aside: riverine scratch
Patch black bulk

The original's in her eyes
My lenses the vexes of [her body of [writing



She's a gardener [grafter
She grows tropes [vibrancies [aural sculptures

In the concentric jungle peel air petallic the far
   reaches of her body

Stumble on the peaking orchids in the dark a creamy
   blossom

Chuting in the sporous breeze find her
Shedding wishes making autumn under the wishing
   tree

You aborted us
I buried us alive

While still drinking at the fountain
The slow livers

Infinity's open book [faced away



You my mirage [me simile

I call me you
Trap me in my child I adore you
Turn me into stone I break you
I ask you to be transparent
Show me I am my other halves



Halt, hound
The trail's around
Scent's your own
Teeth ingrown



'My dear'
I address her
[She has been expensive

'Compulsion's a good aphrodisiac'
'Don't throw me off my own scent'
'Love as disengagement'
[But quoteworthy


She was also my Verlaine
Among others

Having branded her I
put her in my menagerie

She began to compete I
ridiculed her back
into the ordinary


Show me the berries, she said

I'll show you Black
and Blue

Straw
To darn your smile

Raspberries
for your voice

Nothing's too personal
The word my person [l

And you so private you keep
yourself from yourself

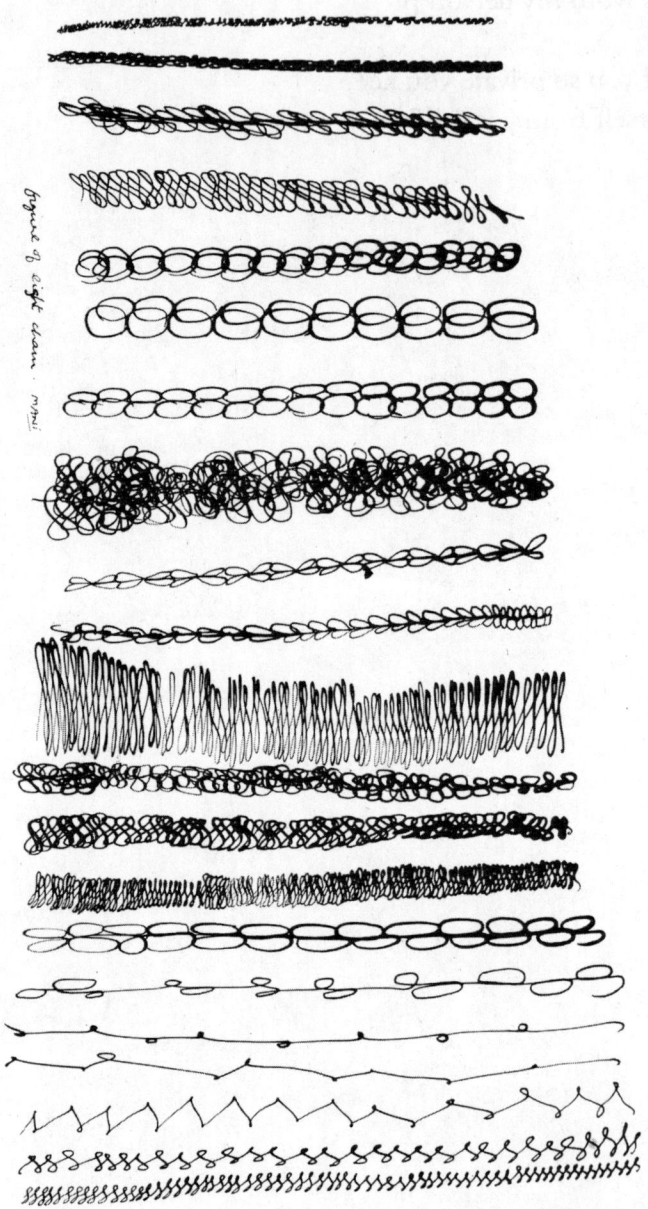

# Story Moon

Pair of lovers coupled
with a full moon—
Formula for romance.

Silhouetted faces cradled
in a generous moon curve—
Pregnancy.

The same pair walking on a beach, skies overcast,
moon skidding on footprints—
Death, or death
rescued by separation.

If there is no moon, oh no moon, there is no
moon at all, where is the moon, there is no
moon, honey, there is no moon, no
moon, and saying it again conjures no
moon what's a poet to do
without moon

# If It's Any Consolation

To you who loved and could not speak of it,
lost something no one knew you had.

To you who find yourself abruptly weeping
in public with no legitimate explanation.

To you who told a friend who said 'this too will pass'.
This did not. This carved a hole within your chest.
There this lives and owns your face.

To you who denied yourself and have no one else
   to blame,
Surrendered to bondage thinking it your place.

You went by the book, did not know better,
   that piety was false, it was too late,

Two-minute silence.

# Waiting For Gold

Long long ago very very long ago
When this star was in that constellation

Men and women were equal
Cobbler could be king

According to Surya Siddhanta
The golden age will return

When planets line up along the ecliptic
In Pisces just before Aries

On a new moon day in Phalguni—
Quote this poem then

# Poem For a Librarian

Big library in our small town. So many floors and wings, we had three elevators and five stairwells.

Books were stacked by subject. Where to put a book was my call. Art or Architecture, Classics or History, Theology or Religious Studies, ask me.

One ordinary day, a new book landed on my table. Called *Female*, the cover said 'non-fiction'. I put it under Gynaecology.

I could not sleep that night, and the next day I moved it to Anthropology. An hour later, decided it was Genomics.

This went on. Again, again, and again. Sociology. Psychology. Earth Sciences. Then it happened.

Inspiration is always sudden, and just as I was brushing my teeth, I nearly said it aloud—Performing Arts.

Over breakfast, I told my wife what I was thinking. She hated it. Glinting, she said that I meant Real Estate.

I know you want to know how this ended. Well, I put it under Politics. And left it there.

# What Are Grown-Ups Made Of

What are grown-ups made of
Does anyone know

Hums and haws
Umpteen flaws

Nose in the air
Hiding despair

Tries so hard, but
doesn't

have a favourite
cookie

# Were I A Wizard There Would Be

Grilled cheese sandwiches ready-
-to-eat on trees. Crisp French fries
instead of beans.

All dentists in jail, teeth
made of steel

We'll keep our moms, just wave
wands to make them nicer

# Doobie Doobie Doo

Oh those
Chairs in a jagged circle

Someone's boyfriend who did not
know the art of inhalation,

morose, wanting
conversation

The rest of us buzzards
and baloos

Wet-whiskered
roaches

**be** the sun be
do the cat **do**

**be** the branch be
do the moon **do**

**be** the leaf be
do the dew **do**

**be** the mouth be
do the spout **do**

# If We Live Long Enough, We Shall

One day we shall
all find

our Orphan-age
Ordained we shall

be sworn
brothers, sisters

Weep we shall
hang sighs

in vacuum,
our new home

You were never there, brother
You too busy sister

Witnesses to the same
split skies our stories same

Promises,
Promises,

# Vers Libre

When I walked into a poem
and met a meticulous metre

Got battered by drums
that drowned the lyrics

I couldn't tell the theme
for the scheme and

bum-rush end-rhymes
crashed my dreams

Maybe I ought to mince
my words, toe the line

But I don't
I'm a freedom fighter

# Conditions of Freedom

You can say air is bound to earth
or has found its use and breathe
in gratitude

Ask if a river is choked by the banks
or propelled, longing for the ocean

Clock hands remain in orbit
by design, it's how we keep time

No child complains
of a parent's lap

When wings are ready
the bird has flown

# A Little Secret

Once upon a time our deities lived in sancta sanctorum.
A lamp on either side highlighted their cheekbones.
Milk baths soothed their skin tones, and camphor stroked
the insides of their elbows.
How we wriggled into queues, balanced on toes,
craning necks to intercept Compassion—
May a drop fall upon us, me in particular.

Once upon a time encircled by nine mountains
where the soil shimmered, we dug and found
the marker for the very womb of creation.
In search of perfection among pebbles,
we claimed a Saligramam.

Now look, the deities are out like clock towers.
Adiyogi competes with the mountain's profile.
He is everybody's backdrop and buddy.
Beneath a Prussian blue sky
to all the shooting stars we reply with selfies.

Every lane has its own Ganesh.
Best means biggest, and the best can only
be hosted on the chief minister's lane.
Poverty dances to free hooch. Remove all obstacles,
we cry, and the electric grid is turned off
so the giants can be towed to sea.

This is the hill where Hanuman paused.
He stands again, high above the Deodar trees
commemorating our glorious history.
We pay homage from across the valley.
See that little structure at his feet,
that's an ancient temple where
a forest-dweller does puja daily.

This Hanuman's ready to strike, flourishing a mace.
That Hanuman muscular, his legs like lightning bolts.
Every statue of Hanuman taller than his predecessor.
Outdone by the neighboring town we added
a taller parasol, proved just who's more devout.

What does my silver hair know, what
do my grey lashes hide.
Slower each day I water the plants,
muttering secrets.
But there's one little secret I
will share: God is a shy bird

So hush.

# Fusion 2024

When the goddess of fortune rang our doorbell
she was taller than we'd known. Her tiara tore
the cobweb nest and spiders on the mantle fell

Into the hot oil of lamps splattering the floral floor-art.
Awaiting witches on brooms and bugs in boots
this Halloween.

Upon our lotus-cushion she took her place,
granted every trickster their treat.
Her pet-owl hooted who's who.

At home in heaven 'n hell,
This Diwali, this Halloween.

—

*Some years, Diwali and Halloween occur on the same night.*

# Postcard from India

Greetings from our penthouse terrace
with a view of the mountains and temple.

When you visit we'll sit in the hammocks
and sip a fresh infusion of Tulsi
while temple-speakers blow us mantras.

Translucent roofing lets in the sun
for the plants, but we have fans
and can move inside into AC.

Everything is now available here,
thanks to online shopping we are spared
exposure to pushy crowds and

bad handling practices. We have it all.
Pressure washer, patio scrubber, herbal
insecticides. Always on the lookout for more

efficient masks. No clothes dryer though.
As I said, there is the sun.
We had to train the staff a bunch.

Used washcloths to a separate section of the clothesline.
Buckets for chemicals marked with hashtags.
Fresh mop-water from room to room.

First thing in the morning, our driver wipes
the front gate with bleach. 'All-rounder', he
even cleans fans if we ask him to.

We taught our cook how to make pasta.
How sauté does not mean fry.
(I discreetly inspect her nails.)

It's hot. My heels are cracked, but
cold-pressed coconut oil soothes.
I wear my kung fu shoes in the house.

It's hot. Too dusty to go walking
and always too much trash, so I don't.
I can no longer sit cross-legged to meditate.

My dear, I close my eyes and recall
how much you wanted to do service
in the slums of Bombay.

# Iowa Romancing

Stretched on the swing at Shambaugh, hands
   squirreled shirts.
Across Clinton Street streaked moon-spanked dorm
   geese.
Hoarse hostel boys yelled back—from trees? —
   'Encore! We love you!'

Broken-winged from marriages that had gone on
   too long, two
Vegan amputees drove solemnly to Macbride Raptor
   Park.
'Hey who's stuffed?' said Bald Eagle Lofty and shat
   specially.

Four in the audience at Marshalltown Public Library.
The librarian, the lady who laid out cookies, and a
   brave couple
out on their first date. I did the love poems; they
   bought a book.

# This Week's Mosquito

Monday when you buzzed my skin was warm.

Tuesday, you landed. I blew you off, you flew.
Go chew thread, you one-week wonder.
Like Sherlock I flashed back after your act. The soft landing on a
   hair, how your lightning proboscis siphoned tank-full before
   I thundered.

Bloody Wednesday. You lurched, we locked
eyes mid-air.

Thursday you rode, rode on my fuel.
Sipped nectar, surveyed water.

Friday I contemplated on give and get
in forgive and forget. Did you drop eggs?

What was the Saturday visit about—
Blotchy, frontal, pensive

Up you rose and toppled
into the open-jaw trashcan.

As duly noted, Sunday.

# War

Coffee-drinkers find tea pointless.
Not much more than a hot water hobby.

Tea-drinkers find coffee bitter.
Like the emperor-has-new-clothes story.

Tea people note how coffee people can talk,
Guatemala to Colombia, Egypt to Ethiopia.

Coffee people think tea people fake
culture, accents and even tastebuds.

Was coffee smuggled to India in the beard of a pirate?
Tea invented so Chinese monks could stay awake
    to meditate?

Then it was Darjeeling tea versus coffee from Ooty.
Now it's Tulsi-ginger-cardamom Matcha versus
    Buttermilk-soaked Turmeric Ashwagandha Latte.

There's a vacancy for a referee,
but everyone's enlisted—
Coffee, or Tea.

# Finding Family

If family is an adverb
what verb does
it describe?

'Famish,' you said.

That's what families
are made of.

Lunches and dinners.
The famished gatherings.

Now I know why I
shun the clan—

the proforma niceties
eating duties

at weddings, baby showers
death anniversaries.

Why I meet friends
at restaurants

Famishedly.

# Safe

When I tell my mother
I'm going someplace
She warns me

Of crocodiles that look like logs
Mountain lions behind rocks
Lonely roads and rakes
Tall grass, irritated snakes

One must never enter caves
Or go to the restroom
in large malls solo
She speaks without
word breaks

No wonder I am so fearless
All the panic safe with her

# Transfusion

All comes down to the galactic
whorls of a fingertip

As if smoothing out
a creased life line

I stroked her palm
all night

Not a wink

Her eyes pinned
to the blood-bottle

Bead by bead
rolled like a rosary

My mother and I
Silent

Her tongue had lost its taste
Mine, its poison

# On Your Lost Taste of Banganapalle

Lunchtime at the school across, greedy chipmunks about
with catapults and paws
We're the house with the high gate, walled garden and
the one tree loaded with mangoes

You never napped. If you left your rocking chair in the portico
you were never far, caught every scrape, glinted
when a grass blade snapped
If the sun moved the shadows, they were preapproved
If a stalk shook you exploded
like a mother-crow foiling a cosmic heist
Your expletives sent raiders packing,
made premature mangoes blush

One day some monkeys surveyed the scene, nonchalant
Still green, but here and there some pendants shone
Next morning, you plucked the tree of all its booty
to let it ripen in burlap and straw

'Banganapalle.'

Subtler than Alphonso, bigger than Badami,
more polite than Rasaalu, sweet not cloying
This mango's named after our hometown
and now the town is known by it

What's life without taste, you always say,
Say it again this summer
Eat your mangoes without comment
Sweet memories, die-hard

# Without Touching

Unless by heart is meant the anatomical,
believers do not use the word
in poems. Believers of

Precision, we
who measure words, distances
between words and things
they try to touch.

Calibrating thus I walked to the riverbank
where countless hearts of stone
protested the analogy.

I picked up one and a cold wave
tore along my arm to crash, not left
of centre, but in the exact center
of my chest. Then froze into a knot.

Hearts sink because blood is thicker than water.
Don't I keep on searching for that heart of gold.
The day I stepped upon a broken heart barefoot.

Upon a rock, a heron, and another heron,
upside down, immersed in the water
without touching.

Then without warning soared
my winged heart.

# The Dotted Line

How many oceans—
A real question in schools.

The answer is four, five, or one, depending
on your vintage and philosophy.

We know Canadian gulls unwittingly deported
in the spray of Niagara, held in U.S. custody.

Of Hong Kong dogs that crossed the line,
and vanished in mainland eateries.

Said a whale to its calf, don't go too far,
watch where you jump.

I'm a little concerned, the southern ocean
is now called the Southern Ocean.

# Advanced Lessons

When their tummies growl for prasad,
my kids sit up straight in bhajans
and clap in sync.

Though their skies rain nouns
—Love! Truth! Justice!—
my students use verbs.

Bypassing clenched fists, their
conscientious poems get published
in conscientious journals.

What bowing does not make humble—
What smiling does not make happy—
They fake now
what life makes later.

# Writing on the Wall

On the heels of the siren
A hissing undertow

Back-bending sea-oats
Palm fronds frisked
Static in the aquarium

White knuckles on the horizon surely
higher than our roof

Horseshoes hung down on the beach
Will cavalry recede

Between magnet shore and magnet moon
Won't ocean float

Sorry fish so sorry garden

A fist mounted the ocean and scrawled on the promenade:
Equality

# No Souvenir

After the hurricane, scour
the sand for wholeness
in seashells

Chips and shards mirroring
breakers and stars, they're
security, eyes of the beach

Face down snug
insignia on their back, they
carry the world, do not touch

Ears blown
Spine spiralx posed
Toss back to the breeze

# April 13, 2006

The way the tornado wailed
Lips to the rim

Flower and needle
Unsheathed tip

Curling growl
as it landed

Shaking in the basement
We ate the smell

We wept

Wept for it
Wept for us

for days on our knees begging
for a photograph intact

among the toothpicks

# Death Has My Back

But for that biker in my rearview
I'd be solo into the sunset,
radio spilling 'road-to-nowhere'—

Can't shake him off,
so I say, 'Creditor, star-dog,
come closer, be done.'

Then toss a wrapper
into the wind flapping
at his face.
Respondez s'il vous plait!

Instead, the road revs, infested,
Countless riders pass us—
steady, sweet pair.

# See, No Leaves

Moments before winter this tree
pulls in its poems. Drops displays
of abundance, each leaf uniquely
boned, incisive edges, raw.

Rust red saffron ochre habits
presage unmindful nakedness.
Forehead clear ear-piercings vacant eyes
blank buddha face carapace.

Sun settles a dusky sky.
Wind blows any which way.
Exhale inspirations, like smoke
uncoiling into space.

There is no event, no thing to be seen.
Catching a scent some visitors go
from room to room ringing bells—
greeted by the silence of turtles.

# Pathetic Fallacy

Sunset sky

Youth gone
Passion lingers

# Law of Physics

Entering the prism of time,
black hair emerges
on the other side

as a palette of gray,
then vanishes
in white light

# Suraj, the Boatman

When it's time
it's time
Who am I to say

All of Kashi's
a smashaan it's
business as usual

I row—
bodies bundles
Nothing special

Mom's the Dom
Traffic Controller
Keeper of Fire

Extra busy today
with what washed up
on the bend

# Kashi Triptych

Don't ask who's cooking tonight

at Harishchandra and Manikarnika
kitchens of Kashi

Shroud tears, skin sears
Juicy fat's oblation

Did marrow fizz
Fire laugh

In three hours and a half
this human log

collectable
in a dustpan


For the first time I think to
count your eyelashes

to pluck them
before they're singed

Of each I'll make a
boat unmoored

Where in the worlds
are you

As if I poured a sky
of wax on you

Everywhere you are not
your exact absence


In Uttarkashi

where sun dives and
pirouettes

and fish roll their eyes
dodging

tangled light doodles
we cup our hands

and drink Ma Ganga
infused

with arias of swans and
undertones of glaciers

Sweetness rises
Air floats sinless


In Kashi where

shadows hover anxious
like dogs marking

corners of terraced ghats
as lovers drink mirrors

a curly soot rains
upon the free bereft

and pundits claim
ashes still warm

from midnight pyres
for altar coffers at dawn

Hey Vishwanath of Kashi
O' Mt Alchemy

Here I am, weightless
Now take me home



So long as mountains meditate
this river will be wet

So long as boatmen paddle
a lullaby for the dead

before sun strikes
and water turns cold

We row to a spot
churning upstream

Hand your ashes over
to the current


Ash can't swim

Hangs on to algae on hulls
Falls into arms of corals

Scraped and bitten by fish
Shat along gorges and flats

Why else do river beaches shine
What is mica made of

# Not For Sale

Our front door faces south.

Not in Agni's corner but
we cook wonders

in our kitchen
northwest.

All beds face north
and yet we sleep deep

and wake up bright.

She watches.
She is all directions.

In our house of the omnipresent
we are more than vaastu compliant.

# Tiruvannamalai

After I spat out sweet-n-sour stories
under the tamarind tree

Old photographs at Ramana's cave
looked at me infinitely

Agape I walked on barefoot
rocks rumbling replies

Arunachala, red mountain,
your silhouette lines my dreams

Every morning, humanity snakes
around you, churning

# Of the Monkeys of Vrindavan

If you wear glasses, beware the monkeys of Vrindavan.
Quick on the take, these three-foot sprinters confiscate
   complacency.

To whom will you plead your case, naked face, asks a Gopi.
Don't you know our crooked boyfriend's really the Prince
   of Thieves?

Ask the dancing trees moist centuries' evergreen memories.

Hurry down alleys blurry for darshan.
Like a river you can only go to sea.

Still looking for your glasses without your glasses? A
   ragman taunts.
How will you identify him unless you become anonymity?

Ask the dancing trees moist centuries' evergreen memories.
Skirts of Gopis crest and swirl like oceans to flute-moon.

In through the gates of birth arrives dog unconditional love.
Deny the hug and one more chance awaits by the door of
   death.

You make it in time. Curtains open dazzling.
Love's blind, and your heart's stolen.

# I Talk to Myself—I Talk to You[1]

*This poem-essay was written for the anthology* Desde Hong Kong—Poets in Conversation with Octavio Paz. *Paz had a lifelong interest in the Marquis de Sade's writings, and I began there. Moreover, all speakers past, present and future can only be in conversation with each other. So, Paz speaks, Sade replies, and others take their turn, everyone listening to each other. At the time of writing this, I was also reading poems by P.K. Leung, a poet-friend in Hong Kong who died in 2013.*

———

Paz:    Man is inhabited by silence and space
          How to sate his hunger,
          How to populate his space?
          How to escape my own image?[2]

**Sade via Madame de Saint-Ange:** By repeating our attitudes and postures in a thousand different ways, they infinitely multiply those same pleasures for the persons seated here upon this ottoman. Thus everything is visible, no part of the body can

---

1  Published in the anthology *Desde Hong Kong—Poets in Conversation with Octavio Paz* (Hong Kong: Chameleon Press, 2014).

2  Octavio Paz, 'The Prisoner', translated by Eliot Weinberger, in *An Erotic Beyond: Sade* (New York and London: Harcourt Brace & Company, 1998), p. 5.

remain hidden: everything must be seen; these images are so many groups disposed around those enchained by love, so many delicious tableaux.[3]

Celan: I hear that they call life our only refuge.[4]

Faiz: Never mind if there'll be no wine in hell—
At least the preacher will be nowhere around.[5]

Chitre: Will I ever find heaven's fucking light?[6]

Paz: Perhaps, behind that door
There is no other side.[7]

Symborska: So he's got to have happiness,
he's got to have truth, too,
he's got to have eternity—
did you ever![8]

---

3 The Marquis de Sade, translated by Richard Seaver and Austryn Wainhouse. *Justine, Philosophy in the Bedroom, & Other Writings* (New York: Grove Press, 1990), p. 203.

4 Paul Celan, 'Schneepart', translated by Michael Hamburger, in *Selected Poems* (London and New York: Penguin, 1996), p. 331.

5 Faiz Ahmed Faiz, 'Quatrain', translated by Shiv K. Kumar, in *Selected Poems*, New Delhi: Viking, 1995), p. 91.

6 Dilip Chitre, 'Will I Ever Find', *As Is, Where Is* (Mumbai: Poetrywallah, 2014), p. 236.

7 Octavio Paz, 'Reading John Cage', translated by Eliot Weinberger, in *The Collected Poems*, p. 237.

8 Wislawa Symborska, 'No End of Fun', translated by Stanislaw Baranczak and Clare Cavanagh, in *View with a Grain of Sand—Selected Poems* (Great Britain: Faber & Faber, 1996), p. 60.

Paz:    Nirvana is Samsara,
        Samsara is not Nirvana[9]

P.K.:                if one day
             you find
                 a more spacious
                     more tolerant
                         happy land

             a more civilized
                 peaceful and resilient garden
                     I'll be glad to watch you go.[10]

---

9 Octavio Paz, 'Reading John Cage', translated by Eliot Weinberger, in *The Collected Poems*, p. 237.

10 P.K. Leung, 'At the Grave of Mr. Cai Jiemin', translated by Yau Wai Ping, in *Travelling with a Bitter Melon* (Hong Kong: Asia 2000, 2000), p. 337.

# I, Lorine Niedecker

This poem-essay catches glimpses of Lorine Niedecker's life and poetics using only words from her poetry. The essay was published in *Interim* journal in 2011, along with a lengthy note and 133 endnotes. Even without the endnotes, these pages may be delightful, especially for those who love Niedecker's ideas of a 'condensary'.

# I Lorine Niedecker

My father saw his wife turn deaf and away I mourn her not hearing

water
daughter

soft
serious

a$^{new}$ a$^{new}$

s$^{in}$cere s$^{in}$cere

```
         waterlily
            floating
                lilyLea
     o my
         liptiplily

            I was born with eyes and a house
                                The sun hits
                                    See!

                            High, lovely light    Hey day!

                    My only fear: I'll go blind

                                        saw a star whistle

        bornsworn
        to sound, light
        peet tweet
           teardroptittle
        be dee dove
            round sound            I must have been washed in listenably
                                            pure duration
                                        cough blackbirds please
```

**plover**
Sir Air

**plover**
apt in the wing

**plover**
hello how do you die thrush

things
thoughts

Rock me out

# man country motherinfested

And yet stand up

           Proper balance
          Water, air, poetry
             Urgent
        impulse tests depths

     pect imagist    dull osopher

Be as solid and dense and fixed as you can Over oneself establish an absolute power of silence isn't it humorous to designate at all rainacular novembrood atmosnoric
Silence if intense                                          two months six lines
Explodes

Stevens Marianne Moore Zukofsky reznikoff Cummings Abigail Adams John Adams Thomas Jefferson Villon Dante Hopkins Lincoln Michaelangelo Wallace Stevens Mickey Mouse William Morris Yeats JFKennedy Emerson Croatia Berlin Bolivia Bergen Sweden Swedenborg Leonardo Mary Shelley Ruskin putrid Petrarch miserable Milton William
                                            Carlos
                                      Williams           what was sensed by them

```
Why my sorrow   Paul      Sorrow moves in wide waves
                     Wind widens the grass
                          It passes lets us be
                          It uses us, we use it


knowledge felt
love held         No child no enlightenment

this loud uncovering of griefs
      the uses of grief
        a pleasure to grieve

A monster owl on the fence flew away. What is it the sign of? The sign of an
owl. No oranges, none at hand. What's got away    enough to see me through
lights go out
         I married I hid      carpets dishes benches fishes
              Rotting alewife        Gloomelmed Gloomowned
                                         Seagull has no taste for fish

                   I Compost    with bitterns
                   I give the soil my phosphorus      madness keep

          I shall put everything away some day
                                                       Die prose
```

# Hero know every _____ in neighborhood

Acacia Algae Andromeda Aspen Aster Berry Blue chicory Blue rose Buffalofish Bullfrog Canvasbacks
Carp Cat Catfish Cattle Cauliflower Cherry tree Chopin Cisandra of the bog Catalpa tree Clover Clubmoss
Corn Crabs Crow Cuckoo Dandelion among petunias Dead duck Dinosaur neck Dragonflies mating all over
hell Driftweed Drosera Dry grass Ducktalk Duckweed Dung Equisetum Erudition Exigential Ferns Firefly
music Fish Flamingo Fly Fruitflies Geese Gentians Gnat Gopher Grass of Parnassus Gull Hibiscus Hog
Hollownuts Horse Horsetail Hummingbird Iris Lady's slipper Laurel Leopard coat Lettuce Lichens Maples
Marigolds Melon Minnow Monster owl Mosquitoes Mourning Dove Mouse Mudsquash Muskrats Oak
leaves Oranges not easy to get Orchids Pea-blossom weed Periwinkle Pheasant Pickerel weed Pigeon
Pippisewa Pitcherplant Poppies Rabbits Robinredwing Rose instance Rutabaga Sandpiper Screwy sparrow
Songsparrow Sorarall Sphagnum moss Spruce Starlings musing on robins Sunflower Tickhunt Tiger's
horn Treetoad Tulip Violet Warbler nest cowbird's egg Waterbugs Waterlilies Weeds Weeping willow Wet
muskrat Whoopingcrane Wildfowl Willow Wood Peewee Woodcock

Love them leave them
     gol bee
          fuddle    Piss tilate
                        so long without flowers
                          flower will devour
                            Trim in one place wild in another

# sing to me

*Dear reader, I trust you have met the cast of these poems already, or—with the internet so ubiquitous—please get acquainted on your own. If I do the introductions for some, it won't be because you are a stranger or lack the skill.*

# Sing to Me

O' muses excuse
this non-descript call I

Wonder who
among you apt who
interested

Greek and Sanskrit
A must

I mean not words
Spaces

where two species
      gods/humans
intersect

O

Calliope     Erato          Thalia
Clio           Melpomena  Urania
Euterpe      Polyhymnia  Terpsichore

Magic nine
all-girl cast

Dad a voluptuary
Stepmother hung by her heels

Constant news of half-sisters
Mother in deep glue

When family's this dys
Your friends are poets

Mt Parnassus at your
Apollo-dance

Sappho plays on
Trade for a tradition

Homer restless
Ovid morbid

Blake who met Ezekiel
Dante Virgil

Come one two three nine
Take turns if you tire

You're Kali for Kalidasa
Ganesha for Vyasa

For Lorca duende for Merril
a red-winged bat

Welcome the furies
Alecto      Megaera      Tisiphone

Justices of peace
We'll need them too

Around orchards Grecian
On battlefields Trojan

In Shiva's realm inside
Hanuman's heart

Gods are us

# Peace Treaty

What if Helen died

Cuckold crows
Husband recalls
Body, face, rites

Once broad Trojan devils now
cower in the shadows of walls
Fearing skywitnesses
Quaking at birdshit

Our boy came back
from overseas with a
souvenir egg that ticked

A runaway wife's a rotten prize
Unwanted alive
And dead

# Father's Day

Stop wheels
Hector's hurting
Priam cries
Dusty from playing in the yard, Hector

Astyanax wails
Faint Andromache
Hecuba lactates
On Hecuba's weeping breasts rest Priam's drooping cheeks

Whose guts garland the dogs of Troy
Not Patroclus's

Intact elevated
Body fêted
A high friendship keeps you in good stead

Your funeral games over now
Release, Achilles, release Hector

A man who grieves for a boy must have a soft spot
A man Hephaestus shields must be made of flesh

His heels I'll cuff with my wrists

His knuckles I'll press my lips

Three children walked in hand in hand
Paris, Helen and Troy's ghost waiting to bloat
Priam's been waiting since

—

*Cast: Achilles: death. Hector: dead. Patroclus: young dead friend of Achilles. Priam: father. Hecuba: mother. Andromache: wife. Astyanax: son. Paris: brother. Hephaestus: ironsmith, god, builder of Achilles's shield.*

# My Daughter Philomela

Little Philomela, you knead my face-putty
playdough-nose

You enter verbs, prod nouns
Body, a fact you do not separate yet

Isn't it fun   running in the open
Conquest of trees   wrists   knees   crunchy hair
Twirling in a new dress five husbands gawk while Draupadi
Shuddering lockjawed what's thoughts where's mind whose
    funpark how to be wrapped   Krishna

Arms crossed   knees foetal   your sleeping position's Leda

Every age imposes its season on you
You regardless, permissive

O Philomela! A dog's fooled when lover returns as thief
Jatayu's goosed at Sita's heist

I did not even search his face I thought him son
His ardour manner procedure honoured your sister

Now nightingales, pity Tereus's father
Parent, place the snakes on Medusa's head

—

*Who's why: Philomela, raped by her brother-in-law, Tereus, and then locked up. Tereus cuts off her tongue to ensure her silence. Philomela reveals the gory details to her sister Procne by weaving the story into a tapestry. Procne and Philomela kill Itys—Tereus and Procne's son—and serve him up to Tereus at dinner. Finally, Philomela turns into a nightingale to sing her story forever.*

# Cadmus Is History

Stacked with crawl
The dermis malignant
These jungle skins are one
As Cadmus walks they sync

Don't come back without her begins his story
Exile begins a hero

Above the ground the trees appear various
He looks at the pointed faces leaves held like shields
His immediate hand darts to hilt

What falls is trunk
Any arborist will tell you that
You can't uproot history
History's staunch
Axes scratch graffiti

For details go to Ovid
I just give
the gist of it we
confront what we are we
become what we battle

—

*History: Europa has been abducted by Jove. Brother Cadmus goes on a rescue mission. When he vanquishes a pesky dragon and sows its teeth in the ground, warriors spring up from these teeth, and the battle intensifies. After much back and forth, he (thinks he) wins. Not so fast, says the dragon's master, Ares, who demands compensation. Cadmus has to serve Ares for eight years. Later, after a long heroic life, Cadmus metamorphoses into a snake.*

# Jove's Collar

How nice to have a wife
Who's also sister
You fornicate in the street
Then go home to eat

—

*Those who like to bring up Europa, Io, Semele, Ganymede, Callisto and Leto are just jealous. Jove—smart enough to marry sister Juno, and smart enough to be chief of gods.*

# As Promised Tithonus

    There'll be clusters ... presses ... drinks ...
    Aurora runs
    Aurora reddens

    In the vineyard
    by the corky
    tendrils on the
    stalks:
            Raisins

—

*Aurora (goddess, dawn) asks Jupiter to grant her beloved mortal Tithonus immortality but forgets to ask for youth. Typical.*

# Postcard Aphrodite

Ouranos leaned and pinched her nipples
Gaia forgot her sons lay in ambush
Even before he detached his thighs flanking the mountains her
    limbs arched for the meeting
Half swooning for his eyes leisurely grazing
It was not a memory   had never occurred
He was always so testy (sons can be so crazy)
Recurrent dreams of a blade slicing his neck his blood seeding
    her body
When they sliced his testicles instead
His hands full on her breasts
Jerked a seizure
She ejaculated disbelief
Ouranos drained
Gaia sank



Bright downward slash above
ruddy ocean below what
remains of sky

His pouches open paratroopers

Be anxious it's messy out there
Wind reluctant
Waves nervous

Then laugh o how indifferent wave
of average height & no distinction
lands the prize



Recall that other time when the leaky punk Raktabija
    'bloodseed' battled Kali
The more she hacked
the more he sprouted

Then Tongue stretched
between Earth and Sky

Licked each drop
as it fell



Fresh froth breaks
Bubbles on speed
Champagne-solemn

Water animates
Hands breasts waist

Crimped hair
Signature

Exactly when does she express her face
Translucent sea-squiggle
Aphrodite

Okeanos marks the moment with a pause

Every wave rises
Reflects
Aphrodite gallery


What is Aphrodite made of?

The impossible desire
Carried by rivers
Buried in ocean

You and I know it is memory
Gaia's
Aphrodite has none

Of one parent
Unconflicted
She heads for America

One hundred and fifty foot stature
Shipwrecked hero
Face of commander

Beached on Ellis
Plankton-stained
Gulliver comes to mind

Little people probe her
    Robe her
Hand her a torch
Hoist her on a pedestal
    Crown her Statue Liberty

Poised since then
Open oyster shell

Desire ... Liberty

# Fêted

What does Odysseus do when
the Odyssey is done

Memory's man
House on fire
The story ate it all

Back from Iraq
Busy being a shape
A guard

Sleeps in the old bed
Dines the old way
Visitors none

The front hall scrubbed clean
All of Ithaca's young men
chatting in Hades

It's all about the oil they say
Finite fire

Odysseus, son of Laertes, father of Telemachus,
husband of constant Penelope, family man

A long night
One half in a dream the other half
awake thinking about it

Over and over again of Helen
to the countrywomen

To the one-eyed scarecrow
in the fields said Nobody


Another war-veteran Prometheus

Dented de-fizzed
Rocket to space-junk fell

Wayward washing
Ragged upon the crags

Flooded by the moon a startled thief

From the day he is engorged and cannot hide
till the day he is mute and will not show

In the shadow of the eagle he sees keeping watch

A luscious rested tongue
and thirsts for it

Bheeshma chooses when to die
after farewells, speeches and a drink

Last man standing Yudhisthira
has a friend a dog

The rest are soldiers, trees
Armour
Leaves
Star tips

End of day survivors
count spaces at the table

Face down at the bottom of that trench
Lots of hands and legs


A child-minotaur branded monster
Thrown in a maze

Expect a labyrinth, a story

Alone uncastrated public object Minotaur
awaits a hero

We want a dizzying battle
Dodge! light-footed Theseus

Minotaur froths
Prisoner on D-day



Arjuna retorts:

What do you know, Krishna,
what it is to be human?

Infant, on your knees
Excruciating waiting on teeth

From alphabet-soup
to the world

Pregnant, determinate uterus
Milk in your breasts

Sleeping Dreaming
Two hands two legs

Breath, bowels
Decrepit in the mirror
What do you know, Krishna

# Ding-Dong Bell

The jetty's out
Who's at bay
War-mongrels Hera Athena

Stout Menelaus
Slender Paris
Homer leads the charge

Imperfection haunts beauty
So imagination can rule
Helen haunts imagination

In the centre of her forehead
Bloodthirsty star of the sea

—

*What a naughty boy was that to try to drown poor pussy cat.*

# Iliad Blues

    I like battles out at sea
    Hot spur
    Cold water
    Blood swimming both ways
    Salty meetings
    Sharks due
    At the end
    Level blue

# In the Shower, Thinking of Actaeon

Gaily the nymphs pretend
to man her prudity
Hard after a hunt Diana
flirts water at Actaeon

        Still in the Shower, Thinking of Actaeon:

What Ovid does not offer
What Slavitt does not explain
It was the water I say
It was the water she
Squirted when you gawked
that masked your trail

Your curs fell on you
Deaf to Actaeon

—

*Chaste Diana, hunting, bathing, surrounded by nymphs ... a gay life! Along comes a man, Actaeon, who stumbles upon the nudes and is duly cursed. Actaeon beats a retreat, goes back into the jungle and is mauled by his hunting dogs. Does mere looking have such consequences? You'd think a liberal translator like David Slavitt might have a theory.*

# Aphrodite:

Amorous
but no amour?

Your cock-tip smiles
spurting
moonbeam

There's a mouth
Doesn't lie

# On the Tail

What did you
do

with the bees
Hermes

Every which way
according to
the ithyphallic cacti

—

*Ingenious Hermes steals Apollo's cows and lays confusing tracks to avoid detection. Apollo catches him by bribing a shepherd who was witness to the deed. Hermes was considered a phallic god of boundaries, so his name was engraved on wayside marker stones.*

# Venus and Adonis

Exactly the
accent I like
Olive in mouth

Let's
in the orchard
   pips around us

Promise me you'll
Speak
Greek

What are you waiting for?
The moon won't get any fuller nor
Venus more voluptuous

Adonis prefers to hunt  not
be chased  in any case
Mama Love's
too Romanesque for his taste

—

*Venus is sticky and won't let Adonis go. What makes Greek heroes addictive? Why are Roman goddesses insufferable? Hidden in the resistance, Adonis feels the strong calling of death.*

# Or Us

Whose story isn't Orpheus

You've been in Hell made a mistake been afraid you've got song
    you're prophecy you're God and you're not
Appreciated decapitated
At the height of a party your wife keels over
That you don't want her back you're guilty in fidelity you turn
    gay the Maenads have a field day   Maenads are our mothers

Orpheus starts a band
'The Regrets'

Dark dark dark dark
Tar tar us
Place as place
Grey gag
Absent air

# Simile

    Narcissus drowning in onlyness
    The rest in duplicity

—

*Ovid does not recommend being single. He punishes Narcissus for spurning Echo. I prefer to go with Tiresias who said Narcissus would live to be old if he did not know himself first. Self-knowledge is a young flower with a bad reputation.*

#  Cupid and Psyche

To p on you
To quote myself

# Midas, a Casino in Vegas

Talk to me, goldfish
Where's *Titanic*?

Fancy a gold apple
It's greed only if you're hungry

Lady Luck just wants a fuck
You don't need no PhD in Alchemy

# Poem, Sisyphus

Moon, Sisyphus
Full
Null

Life, Sisyphus
Chain

Who knows how many

Days in the life
of Brahma

Pebble, Sisyphus
On a beach
    Wave
    Wave
    Wave
Polishing

Up there slick
stars who made it

You know how Sisyphus had to roll a massive rock up a steep hill, and how it would roll back down again. But do you know, a day in the life of Brahma = 4.32 billion years. So is a night. Brahma's life of a hundred years (36,000 days) = 311.04 trillion human years. Human life is not manifest during Brahma's night.

# Ouranos Returns

By 30 Alexander is not going through a phase
By 40 if Aristotle is not Aristotle he will never be Aristotle

The next 20 years
Open field

Around the time you need reading glasses and
numbers are leaky, you run into

Kronos
Under a tree
Contemplating
two oranges
Bitter or sweet?

See what's better

When children do not know it
is their turn to love

See what's better

# ghost masters

# Bird Signs

Trimming the overgrown silences of the night
Scissor beaks

It may be early unlit but the birds have begun to boil  buds are growing wings and the tree will rise featherborne

One row of birds like a stem bipinnate will curve nicely to the breeze

One large bunch will turn like a wheel and then somersault  you will see  a crashing tree  root fist twisting up  cumulus head rolling down

Blackbirds will burst a packet of tacks

A stork quadrant will appear with the mythical carpet

Chirping chandeliers will swing in from the sky in time for dusk

# Classic

If everything is impermanent why do you want it

I don't want anything for ever

You will disappoint everyone
Then you will be free

# Location

Hiding in a tree trunk
Looking through the hollows
Firs in new wedding gowns
Fire budding Christmas trees

It was the trees jangling interior bangles
Tigers striped past silently
Rugs on the floor of salvation wood

The first time I saw ginseng I understood the body to be root
Until a slice of what I could only call steakwood

The river swears it's blue
Will carry you across

Soon as you leap in
Fast moving coils
Who said the python's dead

Where is the hatch
    Somewhere here but giant roots flowed over

Is it sealed
    Bloody me
    Will we keep

Gone too far free out at sea why does the water wave as if pining
for the ties of Shiva's braids
The tangles at the fountainhead
From here, the
view of the dance

# Drought

Fruit dump under the tree
Smarting tender
Under the sore why-me look
A drool bedding noodle soup
Worm hitch

Wriggling gone from the grass no winds frisk
Collecting dry rivers, seas

Outgrown the fish juts
Glacier not much more than a hat tipsy on a lite draught

Blood thirsty stalks faint streets

Air wavers at mouth
Toothless the well caves in

Lips do not blossom even if they meet

The speed with which air avages the plump
Yah Yah The eerious ways of god
Hot baker's fleur de mal

# Catching Up

The orphan and the alien met. One adopted the other.
How did they meet?
Oh in exaggerated stories always ending with a rescue and two foundlings.
Did you tell them they would have to forsake to save each other?
No.

FRITTERS FRETTERS. PAPER & CLIPS & FOOD & CHIPS & JOB & PAY & DRINKS & SIPS & PSUEDS & GYPS & PA & MA & BRO & SIS & ROOM & ROOF & BED & BRUSH & BUS & LEGS & COCKS & CLITS & PAPER & CLIPS & FOOD & CHIPS & JOB & PAY & DRINKS & SIPS & PSUEDS & GYPS & PA & MA & BRO & SIS & ROOM & ROOF & BED & BRUSH & BUS & LEGS & COCKS & CLITS & PAPER & CLIPS & FOOD & CHIPS & JOB & PAY & DRINKS & SIPS & PSUEDS & GYPS & PA & MA & BRO & SIS & ROOM & ROOF &

# Choose

They step aside letting me clean their graves
There is a pagoda in the garden where they wait talking
 as I mourn

I hear a voice granting me this
That I can give up my life for anyone I wish brought
 back to life
But only one

Father of sacrifice needs no help to draw my pity
That is piteous

Mother of passion reigned over me
I resent that

Brother of empire I would reinstate
But why

Sister of sullenness I feel for
And ignore

Lovers of the moment I cannot deny
They did not wait for me

Children of untold stories make the most promises
They will not fulfill

# Tensile

Mused at your breasts
Two at a time
Creator harvester of histories
Destroyer resident ghoul

You turn on the suck and flow but how
do you keep them away from the new one the rubbery
amniotic and chewy umbel as they loudly
gnaw and chatter how

the infant heart must be stocked with fresh f & b
and the gut
taut
clean
washed in milk

# Drowning by Numbers

The retaining wall
Fell on the slope
Ran down the valley
Slipped to the beach
Dropped to sea
Laid the net
Blooming net
Closed in

We should have jacked up the foundation of our
    house and put back the map where we found it

Crusty old cat's cradle signed in blood
Engraved on leathery leaf
Our tetheredness

Fat star fell off a ring
Dotted lines realigned
Braying our battleship
Keeled over in a beerbottle

Down with the totem pole
Dinner at Davy Jones'

At the end it'll be you and me saltface
Warm under waterquilt
Carnival of corals and fish
We'll be grateful for the fizzy water
Doe Ray Me Far Sew Lah Tea Do

# Epitaph

Tooth for a tooth defang
Plucked feather mess
Ring formation around the precious gone


We the child of you and me


Two roots anchored each other
Each both tree and soil


Day and night: lips played at missing
Twilight a lasting a las t


Dyad caught in a snag
Vectors pulled
Two ends of a rope knew they were one when they
    tried to separate

Our future sense created a telescope
The telescope became a passage
Our passage
If it doesn't have a passage I won't call it a home


Easier to lose someone to death than to life
The present pollutes the past
The physical blocks the view
The clatter frightens the presence


When shutter sprang
We captured our stuffed animal
Stiff gloat of headstones


Horripilation on the plum tree
One sudden fruit and tiny impoverished seed inside


Those days of bottoms-up hourglass
Now the reverberations the deepwalking


We took our shoes off and walked. The fender became a reef a garland of shells. Crabs closed their eyes like a loud wish pretending to have disappeared when we went closer. I watched as you waited a little longer. The high tide closed in quickly around your feet covered the bare sand and picked up the backwater.

# Star-Crossed

You hold on to this cloud I hold on to that
Shouting the shapes over each other's voices
Everything turns to water  darling
Tired?
Sleep ...

The riddle of the moon has been busted
Tell me why
Insatiable shift

Why we take to terraces gardens
Wherever we can fly silhouettes
Turning our heads  slightly in love
Try on the moonring
It never fits

Your face the shadow of a witch

Sleep on the flatbed of stars
Sleep on history
Sleep in the shape of Pegasus Orion Aquila Cygnus
Heaving net
Someone always playing at Vega

# Sporous

Red September path covered in kisses
Autumn abandon

Abandoning what you ask as your teeth strip and
　　gnaw my flesh
Bruise-clouds flambéed for days
Stained as if I had gone berserk in a perfumery
Trying on too much

# Address

Every evening the trees inhale birds
Swirling back home like a warm shawl
But I still wait for my perch in your arms
I would peg so lightly the sheets of your night flights
We would travel in one mind your old lands my new skies
And every morning you would breathe me fly

# Five-Word Poem

Those love cannot leave alone
Love those cannot leave alone
Cannot love leave those alone
Leave those cannot love alone
Those cannot leave love alone

# End of Scene

We don't see each other any more
        Was it art for art's sake
        or did we get some poems out of it

'Until part do us death'
        Until we exhaust all endings

Finally singing sol o
        Airsummons

Was supposed to give you the white kiss
        But the bloody roses
      At the lorist
        Dragons with pretty eyes

Your body suits you best
        Conducted like a plant
            All pores at once
        Posture of trunk   of leaves  the
                Petrifaction moment

Your  uality
        iolatedness

Careful as you shape the air
Where my breasts used to be
Inhabitation's a habit

I arrive on the 18$^{th}$
              eyes
              lips

2 days is what we have
              Same as 20

Spring upon your fingertips
Pert buds
Cottonwood
Bee balanced on proboscis
Uh oh in a spool
              Now the tips are green
              Now the tips are pink
              Now the tips are white

# Airing at a Sniff

Easy in the envelope of your hands
Rewinding to the memoir
The glyph in your graze

E a s y  I said to the deaf habit of a jawdisc
What's the hurry
The season sprawls

My fibre was coarse
All five: flavour colour odour vibre texture

We ran amok dusting air unsettling
And now bereft jumped on the moon
Straycow
Honeybell
What else to do but ruminate

Come graze ghost bees
About time

# Grand Finale

That we are scarecrows presiding over tracts
Does not stop crows from placing feathers in our caps
And cracking up

Or stop termites pinching our feet
The powdery husk of their voices carries in the wind
    like sawdust

Look there poor dog pissing in the breeze again
Chasing she who does not know fidelity

Last year's clothes are deluged by sand
In the hourglass of my body is there time
Before upside down

I've lined my pockets with the fat satin of gluttony
I've toned my thighs on charity walks
Maybe the highway robbers will have a special smile
    for me

Our greedy pens gorge on trees
What when we cover all the trees and nothing
Stirs the chrysalis

# Shots

Was in the ear foyer
Stray voice

Now sleeps on the bed
House pet

Diver followed the curve of the floor
Did not see the sudden lunge


If we met now I would surely die
And I would surely if we didn't

Everywhere you are not
Your exact absence

Where does it hurt

Wingtips
Eyeballs
Lumbar
Jaw

Are you cold or hot




Suspicious at the goat's steady eyes and reminded of an early
    lesson the executor stayed his hand
If the eyes are not rolling in fear the heart may be found missing
Could be a priest in disguise

# Shorts

Some deaths are well-dressed
Butterflies neatly folded

Some have banners
One ragged wing banging in the wind


One by one the petals bowed
Such polite timing
We gave each its due

Now uncapped
The smiling pod  seedy teeth
The old bitter-gourd
Shaking to be a rainstick


On the contrary when
You are dying you change
To prose
The family finds out who gets what
You are finally understood

# Duet

Yes we did did we
Would you could you
Oh go to bed
Sleep off
Be ok in the morning
How was it my skin
Had no buttons
Was heavy
By the fountain
Overbridge
The radio by the song
When you knew
What if
I don't come back
For a lifetime
I'll be making tea
You'll look in from the window
Over the porcelain bird
Disturb the bread and now it's flat
Next time check with me first
Drop in any time even if you are not around
You too phone when you have nothing to say

# Sequence

Don't keep this story to yourself

When you know the characters re-read the story

One day someone goes in search of the fictitious place in your story and finds it

Did you make-believe or did you not know

I got it from our dreams
When all our dreams fell in line I de-duplicated and filed them for an eclipse

What made a sequel necessary
To know if the story was real

When a story bewilders folding unfolding like origami take a beaded chain place a scene on each bead break the chain swallow the beads stand still until they settle their own sequence collapse your intestines  take a print  install in an art gallery

# Haul

Anchored to a sickle evergreen seacrops harvest sheaves

In the cradle of beach birthing and ghosting footprints washable ink

Dream of true nu sand unspotted by phantom gulls unraided by pirate crabs whereonly clawing weed and biting wind hold body down to lusty tide

A pendant in the clasp of extremes
Moonstone hanging on a thread
Blazing poet


The poet knows she is mere
reflection
Stays with the metaphor
Some respectful distance from the sun

The cellist becomes a medium
Opens bodyhouse to ghostmasters who show up in the audience
They see themselves in her lake vinegar  allow the gain in taste
   the seeping through the cool gauze accent



Sleeping is like fishing for myself
The old customary shoe will come along
Mermaids I didn't see myself eye
A shark scare

Then Kneejerk Stutter Piercingvision

I let the airline flow
Give myself some slack for a slow graze in the deep
Drooling all over the pin  bloodshot
And reel it in

# Slough

Nude the poet has to fashion masks out of his own
 diaphanous slough
Extract expressions and adore each as a face
There is no face only a deft masker
As shadow to body body to rhythm
Follow the ruse this far  this guise  this guile



Slough must be eaten to the last shred
On the last journey tracks made by the head must
 be covered up by the body
Coil to the shape of a bracelet
Place tail inside mouth
Fasten clasp



The womb never leaves a child
You wear it on your back even as you look for it in
 absent-minded mourning

The new skins you grow are slough
But this is flesh—kin—
Slide back into its canoe
Bark curved from memory
And thus dressed go to the shore your bride death

# Pupa

Dreamscrawler

The first five books suck out your consciousness

Texture surfaces on your body

The dark inkwell is infested with flesh-eating diamonds

Eyes at the back of the neck
Tongue jetty
Airaudience

Plenty of room on the ledge of knowing



Often in the shallows
Swollen-headed bright brim
Blinks for love in the wrong places
O for the false bottom to give



The anchor fell through the floor and staked the core
Claw marks in the unwavering sea

# Worker

Pressed poet
Having to thing poems
The lights are off
Speak in your own person

Anon—Nonym—Nymous
Strong Weak Relative Nons
Us Them Impersonyms
Hate Like Ignoranymous

Many master words

Poet—pretender
Light—thunder

Permit no ambit
Even loser's glory

Humility:
Prologue's cunning
Epilogue's arrogance

Stay young fox don't learn panic

That I think it is not to be feared does not mean I don't fear it. I used to be someone. I placed so much value on it I acted humble, prefacing the admission of my fortune with 'undeserved'. How low an opinion I had of myself that I became satisfied.

Art Artifice log away

# Auditorium

Rainkiss

Some frogs gargled in the gutter
Some frog gargoyles on the path

When clouds gathered
The swelled claim—jacked-up blare—
Bellowing cars fractured in a ditch


Rumbling lawn-mower flat out finally
Good job clipper scrakes the rake

Crickets snoring in the threading salon—blunt jaw harpies—
    mouth organs—sawing machines

Clucking from a lizard poised to chirp

What ate a bird
Cat-calling from the trees

Hollow cross-hairs at the shooting range
Birds on speed

Anvil bird—
Demurrer—
Squick—

We miss
They live



Thunder, stupid
Hair-drawing
Air fell back
Void-carving
Fire sprang forward
Did anyone see the script
Those who saw were struck
Others heard about it



A rooster goes after the slippery sunrise with a box of crayons

Riter:
Must scratch
Pass pen please

# Writing to Stop

Writers, fireflies, mistake white paper for light.

The only writing really necessary is one's Last Will and Testament and even that implies a lack of trust.

If we don't stop writing love poems, how can we be loved?

So the cured writer threw all her writing into the compost—the vegetables that grew turned eaters into writers.

Does the tree take you to the sentence or the sentence to the tree?

Writers once communed to work to take their position as gatekeepers. Now fallen asleep at the post, what's there to guard, the raided vault free of conscience, and the community's irrupted impotence pleads not guilty.

Mishearing the question—are writers profits—was a part of the symptom as writer after writer explained they were in no position to play lens. Severed, they had fallen into the pit of relativity and dedicated their lives to comparing this truth with that.

Now closed in by mirrors on all sides, there is expandable space for more writers to play the mumbling peripatetic undead, propped by a dictaphone or notepadpen. Whatever they ear, it's not each other.

Water, flat and earless. Fins sliced before sharks tossed back into the sea.

Boiler mouth, blockaded ear valve. Mouths ladle air. Soup thinner and thinner, audience.

A matter of time before ears fall off. Meanwhile holes can be corked and lobes can be hooks.

Primitive telephones were nimble and balanced, sprinting back and forth between mouth and ear. When the handset's dumb-bell shape came about—*seesaw*—it was a warning, an aid to exercise both organs in equal measure. Ironically, today's bug-sized phones clog ears while being really powerful microphones.

It does seem as though mouth ogre can only ever be temporarily appeased by fame's offerings, or writers who enjoy notoriety would not continue to confess. It's a getting rid of, a clean habit.

According to one, there was a pile of limestone rubble in Giza after the pyramid was done. Instead of carting it all away they put it together in the shape of The Great Sphinx and gave her the job of guarding the necropolis.

Our body of writing guards our tombs and loves to strangle victims— sphingo in Greek—someone please chop her nose.

Sound continues to rise in the shape of a funnel we are digging our way out of, with.

When we have recycled the page and written on the other side of it, we wash off the ink, pulp it and make more. Consumed, our body's a matchstick in language forest fire, patches of ink fertilize the soil, new trees, more logging, more martyrs. The congenital disease, and the curse.

Can this curse be lifted. Cure, as opposed to temporary relief from pain.

Inside the relativity pit there are those so struck, they hold language by its wings and look at it. A child's sharp delight dismembering a butterfly. Language replies, the dice is thrown, the stakes increase, both sides keep losing limbs in the fray, and the impasse is utterlessness.

Arriving here comes with a wild hope, spaceshuttles on standby, tentative about a schedule for a new watery planet. Nothing happens, language is language and gives away no clues.

When the detective hears artists are interrupted yogis she goes to *Patanjali*. She learns, together with the opening of certain chakras one also gains the ability to comprehend any language of any realm, animal, human or spirit. Crucially, this new skill is safest in the hands of a yogi beyond the desire to intervene. Imagine the disastrous consequences of trying to act upon overheard casual banter between idle crows. This corroborates my own childhood unbafflement with conversations between animals and humans in the Jataka tales.

Writers need help to levitate. They seem to suffocate when they don't write. Language is the air they breathe, the atmosphere they live in, and atmosphere stays bound, to the earth.

Atmosphere also holds moisture which acts like glue. Atum of Heliopolis creates son Shu the God of Air, and daughter Tefnut the Goddess of Moisture. Shu and Tefnut together procreate earth and sky. If language is Shu, Tefnut must be silence.

Silent, Charlie Chaplin and Mr Bean become universal instead of themselves.

One, more sound. Collective flogging of sound. With everyone a mouth, speaking exercises anonymity. The cultivation of monofloral bees an impossibility as even the flowers cross-breed and defy isolation in greenhouses. Aroma no longer recognizably distinctive. Faults of the signature too inconsistent to be admissible. Chanting.

Two, more silence.

When the temperature drops suddenly, trees panic; so that they may not be stuck in the frost with their leaves out they go into hyperactivity and in a matter of hours they withdraw all the ink from their leaves, leaving behind a yellow and red dry blaze. Writer, if you want to keep that one greedy hand in the jar, godspeed pulling out in time for a sudden winter.

# Geocity

Zero's round compound
What the zero ate was a dying periphery
Collapsed into the centre: lapsed circumference

If a line extends on its own where will it go
The purpose of a hollow: to contract
Must expand perfectly to contract perfectly
Fall out of space
Awful to be no longer ANYwhere

How to make a bird:
Take two concentric circles
Pull the inside circle out
of the outside circle
Incircle spin clockwise
Outcircle anti
Touching
Separating
Pump

# Bird Union

What's your name
I asked

Omnibird
Said it in surroundsound

No primadonnas among us
One sounds like another of its kind

And doesn't mind the rhyme
It's the art of singing in a choir

Even when singing solo
Petition re petition

A signature campaign
Second sopranos

Clamouring to be first

# Ebru

Up on the water   lake of oil
Up on the lake   waiting painting
A canvas lowered from the sky
To take it away in mortal colours
To air in the celestial pictures
Between eyebrows

# Chorus

You are the spheres
Atmosphere

We know the nip
Your sniffer dogs

You have us hemmed in breath stitch

# Möbius

Glue came unstuck at horizon
We followed ourselves
Wet the sun would not light
We killed anything we did not recognize
At communion a pilgrim offered tongue for
 extraction
We cut a transverse section in the earth for roots
 found doodles
A straw went through a tree trunk
Deepsea divers slipped through the tsunami fingers
 into its fist and survived
For fear of hurting maggots you used tongue not
 fingers to pick them from dog wounds
You the antelope  its testy leap  arching back  antler
 bluff  deliberate tearing of skin aroma
You tiger burning at its neck
You the ignorant
You said if I am the earth how will I bury myself
Goosebumps on surface of sea
Wind tread on water

# Void Plate

When the gates of spring squeaked in the mouths of birds
I put out a hand
Sunflower seeds embedded in my flesh
A bare-breasted mother re-filled the feeder with liquid suet
Fat River Love
Fire Forest

O the knots on Osage for fire to suckle
Sootfaced I stood uncurling fruitdrops

I could not feed the fire considering it untouchable
My only way was through it

The only way to knowledge is through God I had to say
And what   is God   she had to say

The void is the plate
Engraving zigzag
Fire the flare of sound through it
Voice ashen

Is this writing
Then where is my tongue
I've abandoned the pail and pitched my tent on seesaw water

What if I am my own witness
My ears believe each other

# Other

When I draped it around myself I found it wasn't fur it was alive
   and wouldn't let go

So I danced with the bear and got to know the lightness and
   seriousness of its hands

Delicately with cultured paws it tore at my flesh and stopped for
   some other thought


What does a half-wed do
What can a half-wed do
Keep the wound lush
Smile in secret
Stay in bed

By day freckles pop mustard seeds
By night moon glosses grain on lake rims

# Pol Pot

Piece by piece clothes fell skin peeled
and flesh ran in lumps and gravy

Her sidelong glance still tosses lazily
on your hammock smile
Ice cube swirling provocation in your glass

The bones are good to drum with
Tusk plucked and thrown like a gauntlet
Row of ivory pawns
Pillars in war of no ceiling


You relieve the palms of superfluous arms and use
 their sawtooth blades to slice our necks

Shells of infant heads you smash on trees
Oil stains trunks as tears of elephants

We play calm host to your furrowing worms
Rats tentative in our gullies
Radio flies

When you tap for one last formal dance
we show up in crossbone bowties
Jiggling our hips we make the ratatat-tat of castanets

Your raised leg swings the ball of your foot bounces tilting the
    earth the heel falls correcting the tilt
Chandeliers heave
Marbles rrrrr

Our skulls your lost beachballs
Somedaysome snake our scarf or rag will loop through our
    sockets to polish us

§

As soon as you start to read my poem I start to feel
    fond about you

Do you believe in love

the small l
those little fires
    much huddling

two tossed aquariums in the ocean

Love|lies
    All|lies



Outside The Aviary
Two Freewheeling Snowplumes
Interlocked
Coi!
Ploded Verges
Flurry In The Cages
The Sky Separated In To Two
The Nets High Humane

Across The Room. Hair Moon Clouds. Smile Said Between You And I. Sudden Gun And Shot. Eyes Jumped Water. Why The Sidelong Glance. A Line Between Mountain And Ground. The Range Watched. Grew. Not The Size The Lightness. Not The Lightness The Shapeliness. Not The Shapeliness The Sharpness. Not Of A Rumble. Of A Sesame Seed. Itch Around Which Forms Grain. Need Wind Not Water. Light Sway. Upward Stroke. Eye Open Dumbell.

Two Rings. Mortal § Immortal. Soft Flame. Fingernail Size.

θ

Om is a SuperConstellation
Water Sticks Together
Pain is a Verb
Death is Not
Wrong is a Place
Love has No Opposite
Perfection is a Being
A Dream with more pixels stays longer in the
 Memory
If there was no Fear there would be no Objects
To be Blessed  Sneeze

There is knowledge and there is the memory of that
 knowledge by
which we continue to regard as true what we have
 known to be true

The dewdrop knows how to roll on a razor's edge
 but sometimes a
false step

She was looking for provenance to my words as if it
 would help her
decide if I—
I shrieked—Nuts! They're Free, Fell From A Tree

Some
aliens
will eat
flesh
in the hope of becoming flesh

This is a chair
You may as well
sit on it
It's no good
as firewood

∞

Flashfires
Not much writing
Greek plays—accounts of murders done off stage
Why I find toes weird   because I don't use them
Why I fish without bait   because I love jaws

Heart's enlarged
Do I have to have it out
The having to honour what
means nothing but what
not honouring does not mean

Triumph threw me
Out on my ass

Ears blown
Lay throbbing

Tumourtime
∞ I was supposed to swallow

Wait for the webs
Maggotflowers

Gratitude for the gone
Unsummonability

# Calling

A fierce pea wanted to break the pan
The pan broke because the lid was shut and the fire constant
By then the pea



'Blindfolded for your own protection'

'What use if the fog clears when I won't need it'

'A blind man may see once but having seen returns to blindness.
   For revelations you need a seer'



Spinning the spider coagulated in the centre
Quickly everyone slung their washing over the lattice
Glory's fool began to vibrate very fast longing to be stung before
   his time

On a drip tarantic heart red rosary
Love so ft and deli (cloud blossom) it stipulates lite rolling pads
   of fingers lips
Ripe pomegranate seeds in stainless peristalsis
Milking the erect nipples of god for a glass of fully-flown gold-
   rose light




Oh I know you wait for me in the palace
But I am busy with the garden roses
Dazed fiery I take to their cool nectar pastures
Forgetful of the closing skies




Break my wrists and snap my knuckles so
my leaves cheer in the wind though
my body's rooted




Did I ask for a red carpet that you walk into a plantation and
   tenderly sparing the roses pluck all the thorns to lay upon
   my walkways

One of my oars was not far enough
The other a stick to stir with

A ghost ark drew up
A hitchhiking tree waved two bare arms above the deluge

The current
The opening softening wood of my body


As though I have been transplanted in deeper soil
Now the faces do not float past in my dreams
They stay shivering on my skin

I whose legs were in a knot over the title of the dance


Spine recurved into a bow almost humble
Voice jumping to be bowstring
My weight just before you raise me to your arm's taut radius
Shuddering like the bow of a ship ready
At the thought of what you aim me at I nearly swoon
And stay awake to a hissing twisting knifewedge wind

# echo location

The demon and the dog whirl in space, the knives are out flashing, and shame.

She makes you eat spit and he who gives you shelter is already a refugee. She is a carrier for screams fortified with use and he has lost his fuck.

Everyone is innocent, contagious.

Arranged again in parallel lines, my bare feet face the door, welcoming the railroad of time space.

But death is not interested when I am.

I wake up like a dancer into a rehearsed, familiar position.

The boatman has vanished leaving the oars and I am inflating unstoppably into my hollows—shoes, clothes, pen

If you smile when you wake up, if you don't smile when you wake up.

When we woke up dreaming of each other. When I slept right through your dream.

She wakes up slowly, still talking to her dreams. He is spat out by the night, turns to the tide of the radio.

I leave myself in the terrace and go downstairs. I leave myself in the living room and go to the kitchen.

I get together sometimes, a hall of mirrors, swearing different stories, playing you-know-that-I-know-that-you-know-that-I-know.

They are all true, some the truths you know, some you don't.

You look for too much explanation.

I can go back to fetch a better memory. And I can recur if you wish.

When her voice was born for the first time, without her, she became the oracle with the visitor voice. Disguised, in a costume voice. The costume, wearing her. Speaking in quotation marks.

And she became a hound whose voicebox had been removed, making her barkless.

The tap tips. Top tip top tip. Topped up, tipping over.

The clock leaks. Drip drop dribble drip drop dribble.

Shattering on tiles, walls, loss.

Knowing smile in the arc of a pendulum. Every night my suicides and every boomerang morning splitting my head, ripping the tack at my eyelids.

Bury me in a frozen lake, saltless and safe, some day lifted to the eyes of a new person, telling her what to call me as she probes me.

Drop me on coral entangled, hair streaming in the current, rocking on a seabed of pistons.

Leave me in the garden slope, a dial tilted to the stars, on the orange trail as they roll to rot.

Bury me bare as a bird obvious on a tree in autumn.

Was desire meant to be saved, kept alive, unanswered? But this is a deathfuck, different, the more I dismember, the more I want.

And you my queen of honeylips, the only one who ever knew how to make a ghost of me, play me a new song, recall me.

The nagman brings a daily death, squeezes my breasts, a clay clasp cooler than your hand, gives me fingers and teeth.

The gardener of dust is using my frame as a mould for the shape of future dust. This is how the dust will grow and the pencilling will fall to bits.

The days hatch around you feed their hurried mouths. The years open like doors, one by one they shut behind you; some softly, some bang shut.

Chin glacier melting on jawslope. Long empty breast pockets.

Skin in under water sog.

Unhitched you hurl in two opposite directions. Your mind speeds on, a whistle, minding nothing; your body's best crash, I see it coming.

The sky is fitted linen, stretched over sealine without a crease, pegged to the spikes and jags of mountains, kingsize, navy, preparing to be sunshot. Sooner than lovers can hide, no sooner than the taste of stars striking your lips, one by one stunned and falling to light.

It's all been said and yet, need, blowing between our lips, streams inside a tree. We flowed out of time and back so soon eating eggs our own. Through each other we pass like water.

At the sun to see how it never changes, at the moon to see how it does, algae slipping beneath our feet, roots travelling and dewdrops dying in visible speed. There is no such thing as a circular river.

Unlike bread, the body becomes softer with age. We tag our children with our names, store the plaits of our daughters. Stash berries under rocks and look for them later.

Held in the fangs of a wristwatch, a well-worn path of a nail in our veins, heart-hammered time trail.

No matter who two are kissing, eternity arrives, jelly bean eyes black crystal balls. The longer we look, the more we recognize and anything we could say is too obvious. The songs we like are the songs we know, and every song on the radio is about us.

War is a place all thoughts have left. Birds crash when wind caves in. Green salad fields sprinkled with blood and bone. The cigarette drops from your hands as you water plants with gasoline.

Mountains wait on the bodies of reptiles. Snakes run from burning skins. Mountains fall into lakes. The ground hangs on to trees as boats to sails.

Nipples get hot as craters, beards are stroked, eyebrows pinched, faces taken off, eyes recruited by cameras, decades of time stolen from bee pollen and clover harvests returned to the apiaries.

You know a language well if it does things you don't have control over. Bring me the words without meanings, words all meanings have abandoned, sentenced to meaninglessness.

Fortunetellers smile in magazine columns. A mystery hero steals the fantasies of people he likes the look of.

The spirit of a bird crackles in the thicket, your ears dart to pin it down.

You let your eyes flow into bamboo grille, flooding it with your quest, prising it open.

You listen to the sun drumming on leaves, step into the cool ears of breeze.

A stir passes along treetops and spots of damp climb your shins.

Spine arched vein bleached cold shine of a pale leafback, your hair rises velvet.

You pass signs of falling rock, crunch crisp leaves to powder.

We hear the swarm and then see churning over the lawn.

Buzzing so fast it's a wall, molecules whizzing on the inside, making it impenetrable.

Then the bees grow taller, whirlpool and vanish into a pottery class.

Now we know. To walk on water, slower than water. To see trees, move slower than trees. To pass through mountains faster than mountains.

Gust fist.

Pulp pip comet on cladding.

Ripping birdmast, making straw from nest, eggs to liquid gold parabolic orbits.

The long arm of wind reaches down chimneys, runs fingers through silk ash, finds a page of writing inscribed in fire, reads, re-reads.

What holds up the house of cards? Held breath of morning.

Views not parodied by descriptions, allowed to live and die, a cusp, from appearance to dis.

Close your eyes, imagine the view, open your eyes, replace the view with edge to edge identical copy of the original.

Framed by the window, held by both eyes; if you close your blinds, the birds and stars cannot see you.

A bird's eye: Thinning rivers, half eaten mountains, bending lakes, mild agitations of sea fur.

Clouds rush their journeys, just in case.

Back from the markets of lust, haven't bought anything.

Our trolls rally on the windowsill—the leopard who mates for life, handless martial grey beard, taped up windowpane, ancient ring.

Living in the presence of each other's lives, from order to chaos, dispelling heat.

The one star you find and pin with your eyes as I scramble for a wish.

We see the lightning together, gasping, lips sealing around a vacuum.

I watch you asleep, stealing your time. It rains and rains, the tanks fill up and the grass grows inches overnight.

The jealousy because I think you are dying faster, the faint darkness between your lips, the striving for a piece of your skin.

You lock me up to make sure I am there when you return.

I wait for days to see you, when finally you appear I walk away.

Eyes are emissaries, soft knocks, nibs.

Eyes are tongues, mad riverbeds insomniac for salt.

Eyes are fangs, bared chisel tattooing face on retina. Bite this word, lick that wound.

Eyes are the itineraries of shooting stars on the tail of new disasters. Faster than witnesses, slow as alibis, don't look!

Phoenix of mirages, allusions, holy ash, rising mohair soot. Darkness caving into black diamonds. Lashes fan the air between.

Stones drown to measure water of expression, water nothing dissolves in, pure staring child. Soft convex pillows, seed of sleep.

A false door revolves, a roulette swings back to starting position, the masochists bring out x-ographs.

Unfurling, clitoris. Descriptions, insatiable.

Eyes, are braille.

We burn eyes.
Slippery flambéed moon on water.
How similar, fire and rain, the lapping and the fizz.
Outlined in soot, a black curvature.

Our lips close in a precise .
We correct the punctuation , , , , , , , , ,
On the telephone, brief _____
Two subtle     Four much
Object. Subject. Predicament.

Wash your wine in my blood, ripe veins, bruised rivers setting in the sea.

Eat a sponge raw heart with your hands, blood streaming elbows, black rash stain on vampire tongue.

Sleep with fingers open for new sensations.

Into your glass of red, a cloudspill slashing, tasting your colour.

A crescent fingernail scratches the spyglass, arching its back, exhaling calcium moon.

Wings scatter on waxpool caldera.

For lipstick she used a razor, a bloom in slow-mo, her mouth a widening blur.

Blood smells of blood, recognize it. The fumes bring in dogs off the street, begging for a kiss. My heart is smeared all over her lips.

Transparent as a ruby, bright enough to wear, painted in your blood, I'm your new baby.

The tide in your veins is a longwinded narrative walking us to where we began.

Faster, finite, using up the beats.

I pluck the corollas for the red dew. The exhalations. Pearls.

It is always midsummer. The smell of death is also the smell of birth.

Two can play silence. Silence for two players. The time it takes to play silence.

We seize the silence together, own it separately.

You plant a silent minefield, I walk on it, flashes of meaning exploding in my head.

Words—Tags—Tracks—Cartography.

Telling a mountain by its outline, a river by its turns, joining the dots, revising distances, placing things.

Turning points and stop signs. When you know the word for it, call off the detectives.

Monkeys, we leap from word to word, thick with meaning.

Spiders, our words are resilient webs, we make snares in the colour of air, sweet-smelling and sticky.

Please, do not say a single word. Expressed, dead. You have my word.

The sea is in a sweat. More salt, more salt. The salt chain moves faster.

You keep dissolving but you never finish your book, it is a roaring thirst, the jaws of a lion ajar roaring without stop.

More water, more water.

Watch out! Your children crack your heads open, a jagged jig.

Trepanned, your brain releases an air balloon to lift you out of here.

After you leave, they interlace fingers around their own heads, like it never happened to an eggshell.

The world is no more than an old word.

You can go from dedication to deadication, from host to ghost, but I can carve you out of the air again, unearth your shreds, float my eyelash back into the old oceans.

How did you think you would stop talking to me, I never hung up the telepath.

I have not remembered you, but I have not forgotten you.

salt

Keep talking
Make words live longer
Add vitamins to words
Write poems full of You-s and I-s

O


Things we lose are sucked
into a big hole somewhere
Paper-circles collecting
in a punch

O


A dead person collects a two-minute silence—a tax—

○

Careful when you touch someone
The death spot moves every day

○

Meet my parents
El Nino and La Nina
Blame them for
Everything
They won't mind

○

Stranger
Stranger than what?

○

There is love
And there is love pickle

○

Relation ship
Two ships crossing each other

○

Churches
Endorsing streets

○

The right time and the right place
Met

○

This is a dead person in my bed
Fresh every morning
A desire that never lived
To die

○

Counting the floors as we go up in the lift
Twisted hangers on the back of doors
Fading phone numbers of friends
Bones washed in wine and vinegar
Bookmarked with curling hair
The faces of lemons rotting in the grass
Repeat airings of popstar funerals
Designer deaths serialized
Disgust simulated in galleries
Selling coffins with a view
Stumbling upon the neighbour's talents in the
    newspaper
Waiting for the moment when the masseur holds
    your hand
Your dog stops caring for you

The music helps
Feels like there must be others like us

Let us move from lonely to alone
Walk into crowded spaces and be
one of them—any them—
Go back to the same place until they expect our face
Salesgirls, bartenders, banktellers
All the public people
Counters that tick for anyone—everyone—
You know the man who runs the corner shop.
And the guard with no name who knows you by your floor
Give friendly strangers the liberties you give strange friends
From love to rugby to poetry, don't join the club
Don't decide don't divide
Home is where the heart is and the heart is full of habit
Hum the schoolsongs that failed to teach you to love your
    country
Pack up your loneliness and shift it from place to place
Into the unknown
Voices at the other end of random phone numbers
Leave your eyes on in the dark
Stare back
Sleepwalk

O

WhoooSssshhhH
Lissssten
The voicccce in the noisxxxe
The finetuned ranges
Sounds separated—precipitated—
Silence, amplified

Silence is the not the absence of sound
It's the space of sound
The field of sound
S u r r o u n d

The laughing of rats
Rupturing
A stickyspiderysatelliteweb
hymen

The past has passed on
Our old people locked up
in nursing homes

Laid flat and turned over
from time to time, dying
evenly on all sides

On lumplump mattresses soaked
bedsores stained oozes

Alurk in the dark,
their eyes are cannonballs
in a battlefield deserted

When they roll in the breeze,
you know there are animals
inside these fleshcages

Ill-fitting skins. So much skin it could be stretched and wrapped around the body twice. So many things you can hide in the folds of your skin. A disposal bag you weave so we don't have to bring any when we come

with a foreceps and tray, scraping for hair and skin, for signs of
violence under your fingernails

We have to come anyway to collect your souvenirs

To slide the ring off your finger and by the way see the
skindoodles, the buzzing traffic of lines on your palm

At the lifeline no one is supposed to read, scratched over

Lock me up
but make the walls solid.
Seal every inch
of your open bars.

Call that a view?
These are just gaps
in their flashing teeth.
Striped markings
of my slavery.

Like billboards show
things I can't afford.
Make me scratch and sniff
for a few sky strips

Between the grilles is a saying
—freedom exists.
A lie, repeated,
a hymn.

Big cat jaws yawn,
snap the neck of
nothing.

Forced turnings
in measured space
play kitten chasing tail.

# the last beach

BLACK HOLES
ARE YAWNS OF TIME
AS THE UNIVERSE
GETS SLEEPIER & SLEEPIER

TOMORROW BELOW TODAY BELOW TOMORROW
THE DAY AFTER. BELOW ANY BELOW WE GO
TO THE EARTH TO BE PLANTED.

My mother came home one day
without her uterus
The doctor took it out

Like someone heard me say
Let's act it out
act it out physically

I was the baby who never cried
The snake on your breast
who stung you dry

The vicious pet
and yet you held

I shot past her knees past her hips past her breasts past
her shoulders, way past her wisps of hair, those rays
of grey light radiating from her shrunken head.
She had to look up to speak to me
She had to have wide eyes

Life begins when the children are out of the house
and the dog is dead, I said

She laughed
Dyed her hair black
Made me stay

TIME BRINGS CHILDREN
THEY BURN HOLES IN OUR STOMACHS
POP OUR BELLY BUTTONS
DEATH MAKES SENSE

Weightless in your sticky fluids
Too long you kept me in

What do I do with my hands?
Leave them in my pockets
Let them hang
on the sides of my body

Sometimes a voice instead
of being eaten by wind
is spat out

An echo sprouts
on the mountainside

Soon you have sisters—echoes
propping each other

An eye
Two for depth
Ears to pin
The slightest
Slithering
Tongue upon the spine of wind
Sitting here
Attentive
to a snake in the room

The room is
still

Four lines make
a door

The corridor's rails dismantle
in the room

The floor
balances

A figure in blue
crosses the screen

The room is
still

Turn now to a face
with a startled expression

Somewhere
In vacuum

No sky above
Nothing
North South East West gone
Pinheads scattered
Blew this way and that

Light opens
Inside bright lies red
Inside red, black
Inside black, countless tiny arrows

Like all the phone numbers of the world
in the air, ringing

When it's all over he said he'll wait at the foot of the hill on the
   dark side of the moon.

You have walked enough
Lie down flat
Put stonehead on floor
Leave body limp like tail
S spine settle to a straight waterline
Make one important yawn to sum up all small yawns
And return your dreams
Now you can be made to stand up straight in a corner
Bloodbottle
Cutout cop, you're
Ready for the movers
It will happen one day and I
Will get a letter telling me about it

Dead
Thud
Smug as a poet, published
Zed

Then I'll keep you flat in pages
My dry leaf collection

I will not look for a photograph
You're not the foolish type to smile in them
Or even be in them

There might be an impression of your head on a pillow
or strands of your hair still curling around the legs
of furniture

It was not the kingdom of heaven
The gatekeeper was a gaunt man in a suit who paged me
He was writing in a thick yellow ledger and I was in angelwhite
It may have been the hospital robe
The ones that slide off easy to clip flesh, unfold wings
Save dreamer from dream


I'm looking for something that stands for death
A strong, unmistakable sign
When I find it, I'll draw it everywhere
Lie awake in wait
Help it along with a door open at night
and several poems asking
Hurry death goatshead


Night occupied with the day's pictures
Day gone in dreams
One day when I have eaten myself
there will be a name for my disease

Tiresome cupids
their moustaches
softly nervous
the sweet meetings
of their
buoyant bums
and rosewater piss

Singles streets

Eyes slipping from person to person
Shiny black dognoses and their journeys

Blue denim slashing groin to white
Breasts that must be soft and warm

Girls, gifts nobody can open
Circling their eyes, eddies of eyeliners
Fences guarding me from their sharklike pupils

Not my love, never my love

My mistress
uncoils
her umbilicus my
lifeline and leash
she stacks high
and jumps on top

Nobody tug

Dark inside the closed
snake basket

Still
though they slide

When?
    Soon!

When?
    Soon ...

When?
    Soon—

When?
    Soon.

WHEN?
    Soon.

Soon.

Deep neons
empty
their blood
into the bay

Ripples
separate
the light
into skeins

Skeins
have hands
and swim
along your boat

# living shadows

# rubbersoled

dog invisible tags me
fugitive on empty street
sun keeps us in spidery web
my sequins caught in silk
his eight eyes unblinking
sombre harmonies of
sluggish sound
under high notes of
whistling wind
  shadow of air

My shadow
comes home
at night
Howls
at my grave
till I open
my coffin
and let him in.
In the sun
I split open
A seed
And we walk
me
and my dog.

# The waking soul must not see itself

A chinese thing

# So-no mirrors in the bedroom

Daylight's too bright to see in – drawn across the mirror in folds, a heavy borderline guarded by a beast who looks exactly like me, stronger; hands me back a picture of myself, an alibi

The turning silver opens in the dark – on the other side, all my lives – thriving wildlife at a saltlick neatly poured and pouring in a bottomless glass a glistening leech sips and sips

Fragments of glass strewn beside a lake
Beauty and Beast keep returning, looking, asking
B: Is my appearance my reflection or is it a spell?
B: I am drawn to you as to a mirror, my beauty
B: Don't look at me like that, your face naked, your whole life condensed, that expression
B: You look into my eyes, do you touch the bottom? Can you look without feeling you've been seen as well?
B: How can we stop, two mirrors looking at each other?

A new home. The handymen stand around
looking into my unwrapped mirrors
I quickly open the windows
The cat has seen something
Has the mirror seen me?

**Living shadows
eating light
And I a hive
Vast tree
of nests and wings
shooting off**

Tint of black, shade of white
grey 1 grey 2 grey 3
bodystockings denier
10 to denier 100
flickering pointers on a meter
measuring darkness

**My shape holds
shadows like water
No-they're hung on me
like clothes like air
An endless showing of
disguises, no repeats**

I have a visitor I never catch a face
My hand reaches out – he's gone she's gone
Water and smoke, a thief on the run
I know where they breed – on my branches
I'm after the plot I shadow my shadow I
slow down, dilate my eyes and shapes
step out of the darkness

**I write it down: Set the smallest unit of time and the shadow depends on a few materials: 1)Shape of my body stencil 2) Light intensity and direction 3)Surfaces the shadow falls on, angle and texture 4) Distance between the light and I**

I'm a baby in the arms of my shadows
An extending line from murmuring tree of parents

I slide I fly I walk
dividing into roots
contacting

**This must be my mother's shadow sitting watch over me like a bird
Her two slow wings
A grand swinging of gates
Ninja
perched on my shoulders**

And these are the others
Tomorrows biting my heels, pacing for their turn to step into my shoes

Orphaned I'll be without a shadow
Alone
Vanished
I'll be my shadow

Shadows are now more dense than before
Or my eyes rest on them
Seek them out perhaps

My own shadow is a belt - bag - backpack
When I leave a room I pick it up
a gesture of politeness I never forget

Opposite walls mirrored
In the middle, you
A ghost army rises
One side
inside the other
A fanatic samelook
in their eye
A revolution

Ghosts have no ends
no measurements
They scale walls
Collapse
into a lamp
I hold on to my ruler, sanity
Ghosts in the newspaper
Ghosts in the curtains
Ghosts copying each other
Ghosts on telly
Switch on the light
Replace them with shadows
Ghosts in the shadows

Forest Bone Thin
Clean Hair Corals
Blue Sky Flows In
Out This Ready
Skeleton Ravens
Wave Flags Black
Sign On Sign Knots
On Crosses Trees
Their Brittle Voices
Repeat Under My
Soles Shadows Slice
Each Other The Sun
Glass In My Eye

Lights attack you from all sides.
You split into multiple shadows
pale, weak versions
shadow adaptations.

                Sun spends the day
                drawing me
                in shadow-wash
                revising
                erasing

Disappeared into his shadow.
The man without a shadow.
The shadow had a person.
Don't let your shadow find another person.
Escorting our shadows we take them
where they want to go.
Folding his shadow on his arm he went.

# catapult season

The sky is an egg
Friction is the clinging day and night
How can I leave my framework I carry
the plague of the hopefuls

What eats my love
when I debauch

Can he punish the wind
for its infidelities

Every time she makes to speak and pauses,
puzzle if she hides a cautious fragrance

Do you give yourself the vanity of depression too?

The master said oh go
tend your flesh

The guava refused me when I bit it
Spurted blood on my winter lips

You stabbed me
I stabbed you

Now you follow me
like a rebuke

Carry your face like a wound
on your neck

Hero, worm, bleeding eyes
There's a chill open field
in our scene

where we meet
after half a life

Let loose
poison and pleas

After one year of invisibility
you're plumper and darker
like a tree

while all my teeth
have turned black

Raise your rusty hand
and slap me

when I say you don't
love me

Go,
get guzzled
by death

Snuggle into another
ink night

Every sleep
leaves the bonds
of a sullen earth

A bed is a juncture
in the middle
and a precipice
on either end

When I back away
in quarrel,
hold me

Staring for your eyes
in the dark,
I find them
locked

What lovers can
drop their lids
and have the same dream?

When you're gone,
maybe the air
will nestle thick

Maybe I will
continue,
awake

Big big flowers sucking suns press their bee cushions

The air is trailing with tails of sweet chasers

Passage in the field is a trod down line overwritten into thickness with walks

An airplane bends its belly to scatter eyes on the ground

Saturated ants drop down pert stems

Sam met a girl who gave him a gobble and then spat him out.

Tell me something pointing to yourself, she said, like your name.
Denoted by Sam. My history is unimportant. What's left is my
   name.
Hallo, sensorium, hallo, hallo.

Pink toes. Even teeth. Hearty smile. Flat stomach.
All day I thought of him.
We wrote to each other. He told me stories. He gave me a goldfinger.

What happened? Depends on the mood.

Now like beggars they press their faces to her window.
Her ancestors, lovers  accusers, betrayers, orphans.
Her desires. (I look at you so desire. I desire so I look at you).

How did he find such a large crowd? How did they believe him?
The lamp looks away.

Mask on mask on mask on mask on mask on water.

She sang and danced, laughed and rhymed all day.
Use. Lose. Pain. Gain. Die. I. Get. Forget.

Turn me into my twin, she calls, where can you go and hug the
 need the hug.

No pity, no pity.
If you forget it will happen again.

The soul picks at cuticles in concentration.
In the rollercoaster I cling to my body as if I were separating.
See low white clouds posing like silly ghosts with hands thrown
    up.
The sky is limitless however high you fly you know you'll fall
    down down here.
Yet jump into a sea and you disappear leaving a bubble.
Two people exclude everyone else—if one of them should die
    what is the other to do?
Cry, cry, you can reach the end, finally the kitten in the bag pulls
    in its tail behind it.
Are you alone? Yes, the friends I love most are far south.
And then we act like distances are impermeable.
Take your face in your hands and show it around.
Mirrors will keep screaming night after night tirelessly for faces.
Every man is my husband. Every woman my wife. One day we
    will unite.

The great sleep in heartcove
Introduce the heady toddy
Bloody love, four chamber profuse
What sways what—who lives in who

Weak in the wobbly knees to ride an erotic horse
Gathers to wishfulling tumult tempo
Devil stars riot pulsively
Frightened that I die heave ho when I do brace you

Be longing!

Love. That germ. Callous and tender.
We love not. But love what is not. And strive.

Obaidullah.
The primeve in his zany restaurant
by the riverside.

The chat of the chap who wore panties to
walk with a hard-on all the time.  And the music
to sneak out and fetch in the tourists.

Mesmermaid at moontide wagtail flicks a lotus stem

Lucky dips miss heels and battles chingle changle
to oblivion

—What if—
insist the old and the crippled

The statement is the setting
The war worn, lovelorn siesta

DUCK BEFORE A BULLET
AND THE BULLET
DUCKS WITH YOU

...

Po.
I heard you. Po.
I slept with that man. Po.
I had my lunch. Po.

You: I wanted to check out—and if you WERE dead
I'd spite Death, spit at the face of Thanatos by
courting Death viciously: locate a truly rabid
dog, get myself bitten all over, then, in a few
days, die thirsty, fearing water, howling in laughter.

Macrotomic to hear.
Unsubtle asps are not Po.
The long periscope.
On the elephant hiding behind the tree trunk: Forest officer—he
   can't see you so he thinks you can't see him.

Here I thought. I sit on the oceanfloor

The pose of sands waving
grandness

Little fish nibbling golden scarlet
at my nipples

Black holes are yawns of time as the universe
gets sleepier and sleepier

Zoomorphic trampings
the itiner

Soon, too soon, words won't
serve us

Fully unopinionated, we'll be an ape army
of quiet sages

Then army of ascetic apes will nihilate
golden doom of beaker bottom breaking
like the sweet heat of nose bleeding
deep in a fever: foxed, funny,
forgotten

Muted, we'll reach parity with the highers—
horses, cats, dogs, rhinos, reptiles, birds: all arrived
before us

Waterfall at Solomon's High

Enigmatic standing bird
gypsies at a nasty winter

The reckless weed surrounds
whistle obtuse buffooneries

The rockdrops want to run away to
the plains

Love's an ember, nagging

Like a zealous eunuch's babberdash of sufferance
at a harem gate

Scarecrow: who goes there
who has had his fill of eternity?

# wingspan

It's an age wrench
Celebrating with mother at the cemetery
Sad tombstones laugh ... off ... their roots
The earth is tired of being fertile

Emerge from ambiguity like
the jerky kick of
a bronze red disc at dawn

Sink into abyss
folding hands
drawing in all fingers

Between—
our mock epics

Grieved that we do not know
Anguished if we do

Love is a lot of hot air
Let's have a quickie

Then sog in the rain
and eat mud
passionately

Ha Ha Ha WHAT a trip, what a
GUST of wind blowing a
gainst the hair,
what a car JUMPING like a
dolphin, what a simple

quietness

Somewhere the heart cannot
bend

Pain is the body's monsoon,
fresh, invigorating, vengeful

The core, the mantle, the crust
Enuma Elish

Why down—not up?
Vibrance is auromatic

Newton's moth antennae
go zup-zup-zup-zup

Like the utmost gravity of love
in the making

The earth will also die
and not be remembered

As the faint affection of a dream
after the math

My books of poems
Is this all my moments are

I'd thought all along I'd intent so I'd be ready
but an age is yet to be lived
before tomorrow

I want to play with lovers hundred
Know the heart's hunger for belonging

I want to sprout
in a blink

I want.

I watch the fervent night
warming herself at the fireplace

When you smell distinctly the
mind, the water, even
the people

You're just at the threshold of the world

# Credits

Poems in this book appeared in these journals: *91st Meridien, Almost Island, Anomalous, Asia Literary Review, Anuvad, Asia Literary Review, Bangalore Review, Brown Critique, Carapace, Caravan, Cha, Chandrabhaga, Colorado Review, Cordite, Debonair, Desilit, Dimsum, Durgapur Review, EKL Review, Filling Station, Fourth River, HLF Khabar, Holly Rose Review, HOW2, In Posse Review, Indian Literature, Interim, Iowa Review, JAAM, Kavya Bharati, Kritya, Lyrikline, Madras Courier, MAI Review, Mascara, Meanjin, Muse India, Muse of Murmur, Nth Position, Omniverse, Oxford Magazine, Papertiger, Penumbra, Poetry at Sangam, Poetry India, Poetry Magazine, Printout, QLRS, Softblow, Sunflower Collective, Suspect, Takahe, The Bombay Literary Magazine, The Brown Critique, The Fourth River, The Hong Konger, The Literary Review, Tinhouse, Usawa Literary Review, Verseville, Wasafiri, Washington Square, XCP Cross Cultural Poetics, Yapanchitra.*

And in these anthologies: *60 Indian Poets, An Unsuitable Woman, Atlas, City Poetry Anthology, City Voices—Hong Kong Writing in English, Count Every Breath: A Climate Anthology, Desde Hong Kong: Poets in Conversation with Octavio Paz, Divining Dante, Fifty-Fifty—New Hong Kong Writing, Freedom Anthology, Fulcrum, Future Library, Gedichte, Harvest International, Hong Kong ID, Hong Kong Poems, Honoring Fathers Anthology, Language for a New Century, Looking Back at Hong Kong: an Anthology of Writing and Art, Moving Poetry, Not a Muse: The Inner Lives of Women, Other Voices International*

*Project Anthology, OutLoud Hong Kong, OutLoud Too Hong Kong, Penguin Book of the Prose Poem, Reaching Out for Peace Anthology, Rivers Going Home, Scent of Rain: Remembering Jayant Mahapatra, Suspect, The Big Bridge Book of Contemporary Indian Poetry, The Bloodaxe Book of Contemporary Indian Poets, The Brown Anthology, The Dance of the Peacock Anthology. The Golden Treasury of Writers Workshop Poetry, The HarperCollins Book of English Poetry, The Penguin Book of the Prose Poem, The Well-Earned Anthology, The Yellow Nib Anthology, Trash Anthology, Twin Cities Anthology, Voices NCERT Reader, Where Else Anthology, WIPS Imprint, Witness: Poetry of Dissent, Yearbook of Indian Poetry in English, Zoland Poetry.*

# About the Author

Among other things, Mani Rao has been inside a nuclear reactor, written promos for MTV, lived in a barn and studied mantras. She has always wanted to play a musical instrument and do one or two complicated yogasanas. She now lives in Bangalore and Puttaparthi.

# HarperCollins *Publishers* India

At HarperCollins India, we believe in telling the best stories and finding the widest readership for our books in every format possible. We started publishing in 1992; a great deal has changed since then, but what has remained constant is the passion with which our authors write their books, the love with which readers receive them, and the sheer joy and excitement that we as publishers feel in being a part of the publishing process.

Over the years, we've had the pleasure of publishing some of the finest writing from the subcontinent and around the world, including several award-winning titles and some of the biggest bestsellers in India's publishing history. But nothing has meant more to us than the fact that millions of people have read the books we published, and that somewhere, a book of ours might have made a difference.

As we look to the future, we go back to that one word—a word which has been a driving force for us all these years.

Read.